OZ CLARKE

GW00367021

250
BEST
WINES
WINE BUYING GUIDE
2010

PAVILION

First published in 2009 by Pavilion Books
An imprint of
Anova Books Company Ltd
10 Southcombe Street
London W14 0RA

www.anovabooks.com

Keep up to date with Oz on his website **www.ozclarke.com**. Here you can find information about his books, wine recommendations, recipes, wine and food matching, event details, competitions, special offers and lots more...

Editor Maggie Ramsay
Cover & layout design Georgina Hewitt
DTP Jayne Clementson
Tastings, database and editorial assistance Victoria Alers-Hankey, Anna Gaskell, Matthew Jones, Julie Ross, Scott Wakeham

A CIP catalogue for this book is available from the British Library
ISBN 978-1-862-05866-8

10 9 8 7 6 5 4 3 2 1
Printed and bound in Italy by L.E.G.O S.p.A Vicenza

The information and prices contained in this book were correct to the best of our knowledge when we went to press. Although every care has been taken in the preparation of this book, neither the publishers nor the editors can accept any liability for any consequences arising from the use of information contained herein.

Oz Clarke 250 Best Wines is an annual publication. We welcome any suggestions you might have for the next edition.

Acknowledgements
We would like to thank all the retailers, agents and individuals who have helped to source wine labels and bottle photographs.

Please bear in mind that wine is not made in infinite quantities – some of these may well sell out, but the following year's vintage should then become available. Prices are subject to change. All prices listed are per 750ml bottle inclusive of VAT, unless otherwise stated. Remember that some retailers only sell by the case – which may be mixed.

Contents

Introduction

For more than half a century, we've been drinking more wine every year. Until now. Over 50 years of wine-drinking growth has ground to a halt. Don't blame me – I'm still doing my bit – blame everyone else, just like our Prime Minister does. We're still drinking a fantastic amount of wine. At the end of World War II we were drinking about 60 million bottles of wine a year – less than a couple of bottles per person. In 2008, we drank 980 million bottles of wine – around 37 bottles a year each – though that's 10 million bottles less than the year before. But there's no question the recession is having an effect. Tesco reckon that the financial chaos may take a quarter of a million families out of drinking wine altogether. This would explain why those who spend less than £4 a bottle are cutting wine expenditure more immediately than other sections of the market – many of them were only recently into wine, and they've simply decided they can't afford that new pleasure. And since Tesco are our biggest wine retailer, it's relevant to see how the recession is impacting on them – the average price of a bottle of wine in Tesco has dropped from £4.16 last year to £3.82 now.

How is this possible? Sterling has been at its weakest level for a generation. Wasn't the pound worth 2 US dollars as recently as 2008? Wasn't the pound worth 1.50 Euros, but is at a humiliating virtual parity now? Which, of course, should mean that wines paid for in Euros need to be significantly more expensive this year if producers are going to make any profit. Italy, France, Spain, Portugal, Germany – these should all be more expensive. The same goes for wines from North and South America, where the dollar rules.

And correct me if I'm wrong, but hasn't the government been piling on the tax recently? Measuring duty by the 12-bottle case, it was £15.96 per case in March 2007; the next budget took that to £17.52; another in December 2008 took it to £18.84; and the 2009 budget pushed it to almost £20 a case. So how come the average retail price can fall? How can supermarkets offer regular 3 for £10 promotions? How can one retail giant offer 6 for £10? Let me see. I make the duty on a bottle £1.61, 6 times £1.61. Um… £9.66? And that's without VAT. So how can you offer 6 for £10, fellas? **Who's paying for the wine**, when you're giving it away for less than the cost of the duty and VAT?

Well, there's two things. Most **supermarkets' profits are booming**. Wine, traditionally, has been a 'bait' to get people into a supermarket. So price cutting, blatantly dangled in front of the consumer, draws them in to buy products with far higher profit margins than wine: food, bin liners, over-the-counter medicines. When they feel like it, supermarkets can offer wine at virtually any price – one supermarket boss said recently that for every £20 of purchases in his stores, **he could afford to give away a £3.99 bottle of wine**. The people who are buying the 6 for £10 probably have trolleys bulging with other goods all being sold at a decent profit to the store. And, sadly, they probably couldn't really care what the 6 for £10 grog tastes like.

Unfortunately, many wine producers can't refuse to sell at what would seem to be suicidal prices. Every year there are areas that make more wine than they can drink or sell. The wine available increases every year. Consumption worldwide dropped by 260 million bottles in 2008, but production rose by 130 million bottles. Do the maths. If one producer says to the UK, I can't afford to do business with you any more, with your tax hikes and your ruthless price-cutting, there's **a queue of desperate producers** lined up to take his place.

Sometimes it's whole countries that are queuing up. Now, a single winery taking the risk that endless discounting will help their brand (unlikely) is one thing. But many countries fight hard for their reputation and image. **Reputation that takes years to earn can be lost much more quickly**. A century ago German wines were the most revered and the most expensive on British tables. A suicidal charge for market share ended up with Germany selling us more and more wine for less and less money, until their name became synonymous with cheap dross, and all but the least critical consumers moved on. France, still the producer of many of the greatest wines in the world, also makes some of the least palatable wines anywhere. Hampered by an anti-wine government, France's own consumption falls by 4 litres a year. It's now 43 litres; ours is 28 and rising – until this year's blip. At this rate, we'll be drinking more per capita than the French in five years! But will it be French? Probably not. French wine exports fell by 29% in 2008, and look to fall by another 20% in 2009. Which, of course, will mean that there are some desperate French wine producers who'll be knocking on supermarket buyers' doors even as we speak.

Australia fuelled our wine revolution during the late 1980s and the 1990s and I am eternally grateful to them. They over-delivered. The wine was never cheap – its average price was the second highest in the UK – but the flavour flew out of the bottle and persuaded a generation of Brits that wine could be their drink of choice. It also persuaded Australian producers that wine could be a massive export cash cow. Vineyard plantings expanded far faster than sales; honourable wine brands were taken over by companies with little sympathy for such concepts as over-delivering – and now, a decade later, Australia is seen by a majority of British wine drinkers as yesterday's place. This is deeply unfair, because the smaller producers are making heaps of stunning wine – but you can't shout 'Buy one get one free' for as long as Australia has without putting your reputation into intensive care. Last year, Australian exports to the UK were down 17.5%.

Which brings me to New Zealand and Chile. Both have been wonderful success stories in the past few years. New Zealand has built a reputation for high-priced high quality that is the envy of the wine world. She effortlessly holds on to the highest average price spot in the UK every year. For how much longer? Kiwi Sauvignon Blanc, for which everyone was prepared to pay £6.99 at very least, and often several pounds more, has recently been appearing on the High Street for between £3.99 and £4.99. Why? Because New Zealand has expanded its vineyards faster than it could expand sales. The massive, and frequently mediocre, 2008 vintage was sullenly sitting in tanks waiting for buyers who never came. The 2009 harvest arrived – also massive; some people reported 40,000 tons of **Sauvignon grapes being left unpicked** on the vine this year – the tanks had to be emptied. Prices dropped daily, until it was either accept our rock-bottom offer or pour the wine into the river. You know what? I'd have poured it into the river. If producers think we'll simply go back to paying £7–£8 for a bottle of Sauvignon when we've seen it at £3.99, they don't understand **the British discount-junky mentality**. It'll take years of hard work to rebuild that seemingly impregnable high-price, high-quality image. And 2010 will see even more vineyards come on stream. Where are they going to sell the wine? And at what price? At what cost to their reputation?

Meanwhile, Chile is playing its hand pretty well. A few years ago it was unbeatable for reds at £3.99. Then, more recently, it was unbeatable at £4.99. Now, it's unbeatable at £5.99, and excelling for both reds and whites at up to twice that figure. A friend of mine was asked to give a speech to the Chileans entitled 'Chile, the new Australia'. He spent his whole speech telling the audience why they must avoid such a fate. The over-deliverer, the enthusiastic innovator, the uncompromising price:quality ratio champion – in other words 'the old Australia' – yes. But **Discount Doris?** No. Chile's too good for that.

So let's look on the bright side. If you think you have to trade down, fine, but you don't have to stint on quality. Maybe it's a case of re-evaluating what you think of as quality. If you're an Old World fan, a lover of 'classic' areas, why not use this economic downturn as an opportunity to **widen your drinking horizons and save money**? I've listed lots of impressive reds and whites from Australia and Chile at much lower prices than those you've been paying. I've listed beauties from Argentina, New Zealand, the non-classic areas of Italy, France and Spain. All cheaper than they deserve to be because they're off the beaten track. World-class red and white? Try Tim Adams Semillon and Shiraz from Clare Valley, Australia – at Tesco for around a tenner. Blanc de Blancs Champagne flavours? Aldi's Chardonnay Crémant du Jura is only £5.99. Châteauneuf-du-Pape on the cheap? Armit has a Vin de Pays de Vaucluse from a top Châteauneuf producer, André Brunel, for £6.70 that has Châteauneuf written all over it. And there's loads more. I've made a real effort to seek out wines packed full of character for a fair price – not too expensive for us, not too cheap for the producers. That's what this guide is all about.

Wine finder

Shiraz, Hahndorf Hill Winery, Adelaide Hills 33

Shiraz Reserve, St Hallett, Barossa 76

Shiraz, Sainsbury's Australian, South Eastern Australia 101

Shiraz, Sanguine Estate, Heathcote, Victoria 29

Shiraz, The Society's Australian Spicy Red, Bleasdale Winery, Langhorne Creek 92

Sojourn, Battely, Beechworth, Victoria 30

Tempranillo, Wrattonbully Vineyards, Wrattonbully 78

3 Amigos, McHenry Hohnen, Margaret River 41

Sparkling

Pinot Noir, Bird in Hand, Adelaide Hills 118

Sweet

Botrytis Riesling, Tamar Ridge, Tasmania 125

Botrytis Riesling-Traminer, Joseph, La Magia, Primo Estate 126

Muscat, Rutherglen, Cellar No.9, Seppeltsfield, Victoria 126

Riesling, Cordon Cut, Mount Horrocks, Clare Valley 124

AUSTRIA
White

Grüner Veltliner, Domäne Gobelsburg, Niederösterreich 59

Grüner Veltliner Smaragd, Erich Machherndl, Kollmitz, Wachau 31

Riesling, Bockgärten, trocken, Weinrieder, Niederösterreich 48

Red

Zweigelt, Altenriederer, Niederösterreich 73

CHILE
White

Chardonnay, The Society's Chilean (Concha y Toro), Casablanca Valley 88

Chardonnay, Wild Ferment, Errazuriz, Casablanca Valley 50

Sauvignon Blanc, Alta Tierra, Founders' Series, Viña Falernia, Elqui Valley 60

Sauvignon Blanc, Garuma Vineyard, Viña Leyda, Leyda Valley 53

Sauvignon Blanc, Los Nogales, Montes/Tesco Finest, Leyda Valley 63

Viognier, Anakena, Single Vineyard, Rapel Valley 55

Red

Cabernet Sauvignon, Antiguas Reservas, Cousiño-Macul, Maipo Valley 76

Cabernet Sauvignon, Chilean (Asda Extra Special), Aconcagua Valley 91

Carmenère, Arboleda, Viña Seña, Colchagua Valley 69

Carmenère, Chilean Fairtrade, Curicó Valley 94

Fina Sangre, Haras de Pirque 42

Merlot, Miramonte Ridge Red (Viña Casablanca), Rapel Valley 90

Merlot Reserva, Carmen, Casablanca Valley 75

Merlot, Rio Alto Classic, Viña San Esteban, Aconcagua Valley 92

Merlot, Sainsbury's Chilean 101

Merlot, Sainsbury's Taste the Difference (Viña Errázuriz), Curicó 90

Merlot, Soleado, Valle Central 99

Merlot, Winemaker's Lot 198T, Peumo Vineyard, Concha y Toro, Rapel Valley 79

Pinot Noir Reserva, Nostros, Casablanca Valley 81

Pinot Noir, Tobiano, San Antonio 40

Shiraz, Max Reserva, Errazuriz, Aconcagua Valley 72

Syrah, Reserva, Viña Falernia, Elqui 67

Syrah, T.H, Undurraga, Maipo Valley 67

ENGLAND
Rosé

English Rosé (Chapel Down), Kent 103

Sparkling

Vintage Reserve Brut, Chapel Down, Kent 116

FRANCE

White

Chablis, Dom. la Vigne Blanche, Burgundy 54

Chardonnay Bourgogne, Jurassique, Jean-Marc Brocard, Burgundy 57

Chardonnay, Limoux, Dom. Begude, Languedoc 58

Chasselas Sans Soufre, Pierre Frick, Alsace 48

Chenin Blanc, La Grille, Loire Valley 86

Collioure, Cornet & Cie, Cave de l'Abbé Rous, Roussillon 50

VdP des Côtes de Gascogne (Sainsbury's) 98

Fié Gris, VdP du Val de Loire, Dom. de l'Aujardière, Loire Valley 32

VdP du Gers, Lesc, Producteurs Plaimont 88

Gewurztraminer, Réserve, Cave Vinicole à Hunawihr, Alsace 47

Gewurztraminer, Sainsbury's Taste the Difference/Cave de Turckheim, Alsace 64

Montlouis-sur-Loire, Le Volagré, Stéphane Cossais, Loire Valley 35

Muscadet Sèvre et Maine sur lie, André-Michel Brégeon, Loire Valley 63

Muscadet Sèvre et Maine sur lie, Cuvée des Ceps Centenaires, Ch. de Chasseloir, Chéreau Carré, Loire Valley 62

Pinot Blanc-Auxerrois, Albert Mann, Alsace 46

Pouilly Fumé, Sainsbury's Taste the Difference/Dom. André & Edmond Figeat, Loire Valley 47

Riesling Reserve, Trimbach, Alsace 40

Santenay, Dom. Claude Nouveau, Burgundy 47

Sauvignon Blanc, Premières Côtes de Blaye, Chapelle de Tutiac, Cave des Hauts de Gironde, Bordeaux 51

Sauvignon, Saint-Bris, Clotilde Davenne, Burgundy 62

Sauvignon, Touraine, Dom. Jacky Marteau, Loire Valley 57

Vin de Savoie, L'Orangerie, Philippe & François Tiollier, Savoie 56

Red

VdP de l'Aude, Cuvée de Richard, Languedoc 99

Bourgueil, Le Pins, Dom. de la Lande, Loire Valley 69

Cabernet Sauvignon, VdP de Vaucluse, Dom. des Anges, Rhône Valley 83

Carignan (Old Vine), Cuvée Christophe, VdP de l'Aude, Dom. de la Souterranne, Languedoc 36

Carignan, La Différence, VdP des Côtes Catalanes, Roussillon 94

Corbières, Dom. de Fontsèque (Gérard Bertrand), Languedoc 69

Corbières, Réserve de la Perrière, Mont Tauch, Languedoc 100

Cornas, Brise Cailloux, Matthieu Barret/Dom. du Coulet, Rhône Valley 25

Costières de Nîmes, Cuvée Tradition, Mas Carlot, Rhône Valley 81

VdP des Côtes Catalanes, The Society's French Full Red, Roussillon 93

Côtes du Rhône, Le Pavillon, Ch. Beauchêne, Rhône Valley 77

Côtes du Rhône (Waitrose), Rhône Valley 99

Côtes du Rhône Village Sablet, Dom. des Espiers, Rhône Valley 68

Côtes du Rhône Villages, Sainsbury's Taste the Difference (Chapoutier), Rhône Valley 89

La Garrigue, VdP des Côtes de Thongue, Dom. Sainte Rose, Languedoc 80

Crozes-Hermitage, Dom. des Grands Chemins, Delas, Rhône Valley 41

La Guerrerie (vin de table), Le Clos du Tue-Boeuf 33

Grenache Noir, La Différence, VdP des Côtes Catalanes, Roussillon 92

Grenache, VdP de Vaucluse, Dom. André Brunel, Rhône Valley 82

Grenache-Syrah-Mourvèdre, VdP d'Oc, Dom. la Croix Martelle, Languedoc 93

Lirac, Roquedon, Alain Jaume, Rhône Valley 43

Marcillac, Cuvée Laïris, Jean-Luc Matha, South-West 73

Marselan, VdP d'Oc, Dom. de la Ferrandière, Languedoc 83

Médoc, Ch. Labadie, Bordeaux 70

Merlot, Cuvée Guillaume, VdP de l'Aude, Dom. de la Souterranne, Languedoc 77

Minervois, Le Rouge de l'Azerolle, Ch. Mirausse, Languedoc 80

Minervois, Lo Cagarol, Dom. Tour Trencavel, Languedoc 29

St-Nicolas-de-Bourgueil, Les Graviers, Frederic Mabileau, Loire Valley 66

Syrah, Camplazens, VdP d'Oc, Ch. Camplazens, Languedoc 65

Syrah-Grenache, VdP des Côtes de Thongue, Le Champ du Coq, Dom. La Croix Belle, Languedoc 79

Rosé

Bordeaux Rosé, Dom. de Sours, Bordeaux 106

La Brouette Rosé, VdP du Comté Tolosan, Producteurs Plaimont 106

Corse Sartène Rosé, Dom. Saparale, Corsica 103

Côtes de Provence, Ch. Saint Baillon, Provence 105

Syrah, VdP des Côtes de Thongue, Dom. Saint Pierre, Languedoc 105

Tavel, Jean Oliver, Ch. d'Aquéria, Rhône Valley 103

Sparkling

Champagne, Blanc de Blancs Grand Cru, Le Mesnil 114

Champagne, Blanc de Noirs Brut (Sainsbury's) 117

Champagne, Brut Zero, Tarlant 114

Champagne, Brut Selection, Marc Chauvet 116

Champagne, Grand Cru Blanc de Blancs Brut, R & L Legras 115

Champagne, Premier Cru Brut, Pierre Vaudon (Union Champagne) 115

Crémant de Bourgogne Brut Rosé, Blason de Bourgogne, Caves de Bailly, Burgundy 119

Crémant du Jura, Chardonnay Brut, Philippe Michel 121

Crémant de Loire Brut, Jean-Marie Penet, Ch. de la Presle, Loire Valley 119

Sweet

Jurançon, Cuvée Jean, Ch. Jolys, South-West 127

Pacherenc du Vic Bilh, Maestria, Producteurs Plaimont, South-West 127

GERMANY

White

Riesling Auslese, Escherndorfer Lump, Horst Sauer, Franken 21

Riesling Kabinett, Ayler Kupp, Margarethenhof Weingut Weber, Mosel 60

Riesling Kabinett, Scharzhofberger, von Kesselstatt, Mosel 54

Sweet

Weissburgunder Eiswein, Darting Estate, Pfalz 124

HUNGARY

White

Pinot Grigio-Chardonnay, Monte Cappella, Nagyréde 98

Sparkling

Pinot Grigio Brut, Monte Cappella, Balatonboglari 121

ITALY

White

Carso, Vitovska, Vinja Barde, Parovel, Friuli 24

Erbaluce di Caluso, La Rustìa, Orsolani, Piedmont 39

Falanghina, Biblos, Di Majo Norante, Molise 53

Fiano, Settesoli/Asda Extra Special, Sicily 87

Grecanico, IGT Sicilia, Terre di Giumara, Caruso & Minini, Sicily 64

Pecorino, Colle dei Venti, Terre di Chieti IGT, Caldora , Abruzzo 46

Pecorino, Colli Aprutini, Fonte Cupa, Camillo Montori, Abruzzo 34

Soave Classico, Terre di Monteforte, Cantina di Monteforte, Veneto 87

Soave Colli Scaligeri, Castelcerino, Filippi, Veneto 52

Verdicchio dei Castelli di Jesi, Moncaro, Marche 89

Red

Bardolino, Recchia, Veneto 89
Maté (vino da tavola), Sottimano 37
Montepulciano d'Abruzzo, Gran
  Sasso, Abruzzo 78
Negroamaro del Salento, Vittoria,
  Pichierri/Vinicola Savese, Puglia 79
Nero d'Avola, Settesoli/Tesco Finest,
  Sicily 90
Trinacria Rosso, IGT Sicilia 101
Valpolicella Ripasso (Asda Extra
  Special), Veneto 83
Vino da Tavola Rosso (Marks &
  Spencer)100

Sparkling

Lambrusco Reggiano, Autentico,
  Merdici Ermete & Figli, Emilia-
  Romagna 120
Moscato d'Asti, Sourgal, Elio
  Perrone, Piedmont 120
Prosecco, Casa Sant'Orsola 118
Prosecco Raboso (Marks & Spencer)
  119
Prosecco Valdobbiadene, Extra Dry,
  Villa Sandi, Veneto 118

NEW ZEALAND
White

Chardonnay, Fairleigh Estate, Wither
  Hills, Marlborough 57
Chenin Blanc, Black Label, Esk
  Valley, Hawkes Bay 56
Pinot Grigio (Co-op), Marlborough
  59

Pinot Gris, Te Mara, Central Otago 28
Riesling, Opou Vineyard, Millton,
  Gisborne 46
Riesling, Private Bin, Villa Maria,
  Marlborough 60
Riesling, Waipara West, Waipara 55
Sauvignon Blanc, Cellar Selection,
  Villa Maria, Marlborough 49
Sauvignon Blanc, Graham Vineyard,
  Villa Maria, Marlborough 22
Sauvignon Blanc, Soul of the South,
  Waipara Hills, Marlborough 51
Sauvignon Blanc, Tawhiri, Yealands
  Estate, Marlborough 61

Red

Gamay Noir, Woodthorpe Vineyard,
  Te Mata Estate, Hawkes Bay 68
Merlot, Private Bin, Villa Maria,
  Hawkes Bay 74
Merlot-Cabernet Sauvignon-Malbec,
  Esk Valley, Hawkes Bay 70
Merlot-Malbec, Gravel Pit Red, Wild
  Rock, Hawkes Bay 71
Pinot Noir, Cellar Selection, Villa
  Maria, Marlborough 26
Pinot Noir, Paddy Borthwick,
  Wairarapa 25
Pinot Noir, Tesco Finest, Marlborough
  75
Syrah, Vidal, Hawkes Bay 72

Rosé

Merlot-Malbec Rosé, Esk Valley,
  Hawkes Bay 104

Sparkling

Pelorus, Cloudy Bay 117

PORTUGAL
White

Vinho Verde, Quinta de Azevedo 86

Fortified

Fonseca Crusted Port 135
Graham's Crusted Port 135
Graham's Quinta dos Malvedos
  Vintage Port 133
Pink Port (Marks & Spencer) 136
Ruby Port (Asda) 136
Sainsbury's 10 Year Old Tawny 136
Taylor's Vargellas Vintage Port 134
Terra Prima Port, Fonseca 135
Warre's bottle-matured Late Bottled
  Vintage 134

SOUTH AFRICA
White

Chardonnay, Chamonix, Franschhoek
  48
Chenin Blanc, Terroir Selection,
  Springfontein Estate, Walker Bay 31
Sauvignon Blanc, M'hudi (Villiera
  Wines), Western Cape 61
Semillon, Ghost Corner, David
  Nieuwoudt, Elim 28
Tokara White, Stellenbosch 23

Red

Pinotage, Beyers Truter/Tesco Finest,
  Stellenbosch 77

Rosé

Cabernet Sauvignon Rosé, Mulderbosch, Stellenbosch 104

SPAIN
White

Godello, Valdeorras, Clasico, Viña Somoza, Galicia 49

Macabeu-Chardonnay, Conca de Barberà, Castillo de Montblanc, Catalunya 88

Rioja Reserva, Senorio de Laredo, Bodegas Laredo 56

Sauvignon Blanc-Verdejo, Storks' Tower, Vino de la Tierra de Castilla y León, Hijos de Antonio Barcelo 86

Red

Garnacha, Malena, Miguel Torres, Catalunya 80

Garnacha, Vineyard X (Bodegas Borsao), Campo de Borja 93

Garnacha-Shiraz (Spanish, Marks & Spencer), Cariñena 100

Gran López Tinto (Crianzas y Viñedos Santo Cristo), Campo de Borja 100

Gran Tesoro Garnacha (Bodegas Borsao), Campo de Borja 101

Montsant, Acústic Vinyes Velles Nobles, Garnatxa-Samso, Acústic Celler, Catalunya 34

Montsant, Finca L'Argatà, Joan d'Anguera, Catalunya 39

Rioja, Reciente (Bodegas Olarra) 95

Rioja, Vega Ariana 95

Rioja Crianza, Adnams Selection/Monte Acuro (Bodegas Medievo) 78

Rioja Crianza, Graciano, Viña Ijalba 65

Rioja Crianza, Izadi 66

Rioja Crianza,The Society's (Bodegas Palacio) 81

Rioja Reserva, Contino 38

Rioja Reserva, Viña Mara/Tesco Finest, Baron de Ley 76

Rosé

Tarragona, Terramar Rosado, De Muller, Catalunya 107

Utiel-Requena, Las Falleras, Valencia 107

Utiel-Requena Rosado, Viña Decana, Valencia 107

Viña Sol Rosé, Torres, Catalunya 105

Sparkling

Cava, Mas Miralda Brut (Asda Extra Special) 121

Cava, Vineyard X 120

Sweet

Monastrell, Castaño Dulce, Bodegas Castaño, Yecla 125

Fortified

Amontillado, Lustau/Sainsbury's Taste the Difference 132

Amontillado Maribel, Sánchez Romate 131

Amontillado, Tio Diego, Valdespino 130

Fino, Inocente, Valdespino 130

Manzanilla (Williams & Humbert/ Marks & Spencer) 133

Manzanilla (Bodegas Almirante/ Asda)133

Dry Oloroso, Lustau/Sainsbury's Taste the Difference 132

Sweet Oloroso, La Copita (Emilio Lustau) 131

Sweet Pedro Ximenez Sherry (Williams & Humbert/Sainsbury's Taste the Difference) 132

USA
White

Chardonnay, Schug, Carneros, California 43

Red

Cabernet Sauvignon, Reserve, Edward's Block, Napa Valley, California 43

Sparkling

Quartet Brut, Roederer Estate, Anderson Valley, California 115

Index by producers/brands

TOP
250

TOP
50

Some wines just have it – that extra something, that emotion, that mojo. Other wines, often more famous, have crucial components missing: heart, belief, passion, imagination. Instead they offer complacency, arrogance, a nice Mercedes Benz for the producer. Where there should be magical surprises lurking gleefully in the core of the wine, there's predictability. Where there should be expression of the vineyard with all its peculiarities, expression of the grape variety in its brilliant points of difference from others, there's a lazy desire to conform to certain internationally understood norms.

Well, you won't find any of those here. I've chosen 50 wines that have made my heart leap, my spirits warm and my worries ease. An amazing number come in at between £10 and £15. And they're here on merit: they took up the challenge to impress. Partly this is because they do not try so hard to be something they're not, as more expensive wines often do. Partly it's because they come from less well-known grape varieties or are grown in less glitzy regions. And partly it's because they haven't forgotten that wine is for drinking, for carousing, for cheerful chat and friendly food, not for marking out of 100 and spitting down the sink. These wines are a drinker's choice, regardless of whether anyone would award them a trophy or a perfect score.

This chapter lists my favourite wines of the year, both red and white:
🍷 = red wine   🍷 = white wine

1 2006 Chardonnay, Kooyong Estate, Mornington Peninsula, Victoria, Australia, 13% abv
♀ Great Western Wine, Swig, £18.95

It was only when I realized how utterly delicious this wine was that I began to ask myself – when was the last time I actually bought an Aussie Chardie? And I worked out I hadn't bought a single bottle this year. That's terrible for a wine style that used to be one of my favourites. But perhaps the culprit here is that phrase 'Aussie Chardie'. This has come to mean some deep-discounted, sugary, claggy, big brand rubbish, but in fact 'Aussie Chardie' – wonderfully ripe, golden, viscous, tropical – was the wine that ignited our British wine revolution 20 years ago. The trouble is those grand old styles aren't made any more and even if they were, I suspect we've now all become a bit more sophisticated and might find them too much of a mouthful. So step forward Kooyong. This is new-wave Australian Chardonnay (not Aussie Chardie) at its serious, magnificent best. The grapes grow on the cool and lovely Mornington Peninsula, south of Melbourne. The grapes ripen, but they never overripen, and they give wine of an irresistibly nutty style, dry and waxy, scented with a savoury quality the French call 'sauvage' – it's sort of like celestial sausagemeat (well, I didn't *have* to tell you) – and with a soft, creamy texture like oatmeal. If you were truly Francocentric you could say Mornington Peninsula produces Australia's most Burgundy-like Chardonnay. Or you could say, 'to hell with Burgundy, welcome to the new generation of Aussie Chardie.' An Aussie Chardie my top wine. Whatever next?

❢ The 2006 Kooyong Pinot Noir (£19.95, Great Western Wine, Lea and Sandeman, Wine Society) is also absolutely delicious.

2 2002 Riesling Auslese, Escherndorfer Lump, Horst Sauer, Franken, Germany, 8.5% abv
♀ Justerini & Brooks, £19.97

Ah, the delights of swimming against the current. And when it comes to sweet German wine appreciation, it sometimes feels more like swimming up a waterfall, especially when the wine has such an enticing name as 'Escherndorfer Lump'. You have to be very proficient in the German language for the idea of that to set your mouth watering. Let me just say that the Lump vineyard is one of the best in Franconia – aka Franken. (My dictionary tells me 'Lump' means scamp or rascal.) Horst Sauer is one of the most brilliant winemakers in Germany. And 2002 is an excellent vintage. Put all that together with the term Auslese – which means the grapes were picked late into the autumn – and you've got a stunning wine, if only I can persuade you to try it. By itself, on a summer evening – a bottle, a glass and you. Full gold in colour, the flavour is the essence of gold – the last late autumn golden plum on the bough, the intense golden glory of evening sun piercing the orchard shadows, the nectar dripping out of a goldengage at harvest time as the wasps clamour and throb to suck it dry. Mix this with a minerality of genius: putty and linseed oil, shiny boot leather and a dash of petrol. Coat the lemon zest acidity with buttercream and crème fraîche. Close your eyes. Drink. And dream.

3 2006 Cabernet Sauvignon, Balnaves, Coonawarra, South Australia, 15% abv
♀ Ballantynes, Harvey Nichols, Liberty Wines and others, £20.49

Coonawarra – lost in the swampy south of South Australia – regularly puts forward its claim to be the greatest Cabernet region in Australia and one of the greatest in the world. And it doesn't base its claim on the intricate, intellectual complexity of its wines. In a way, Coonawarra bases its claim on simplicity. Many of the world's great taste experiences are simple, but perfect. Bacon and eggs. Toast and butter. Roast beef and roast potatoes. Nothing complex, but when the raw ingredients are good enough, unbeatable. Cabernet Sauvignon is the main grape variety of many of Bordeaux's greatest wines from the Médoc region. At their best they display a

limpid purity of taste based on blackcurrant and cedar wood, perhaps a cedar cigar box. And nothing else, however hard some critics try to complicate matters. Cabernet in Coonawarra has a purity of blackcurrant somewhere between old-style Allen & Hanbury blackcurrant pastilles – the ones in the gold and blue tin – and my mum's blackcurrant jam. There's no greater blackcurrant flavour in the world than my mum's jam, but this wine gets close. The cedar here is replaced by mint – an intriguing mix of peppermint leaf, verbena and Vicks VapoRub – and Bordeaux bitterness gets a touch of the exotic with the chewy twist of Seville marmalade orange peel. I'm complicating matters. Don't let me. This Cabernet is an utterly delicious glass of red. 'Nuff said.

4 2008 Sauvignon Blanc, Graham Vineyard, Villa Maria, Marlborough, New Zealand, 13% abv
♀ Waitrose, £12.99

This wine comes as such a relief. I've been very critical of many of the 2008 Kiwi Sauvignons that have been hitting our shores this year – oversweetened, sweaty, dilute and deep-discounted. Really, the quality and style of some of them has had me fuming. And then along comes this to remind me why we all fell in love with New Zealand in the first place. It's not cheap, but it's absolutely worth the money. The Graham Vineyard is a little south of the main Marlborough vines, in the Awatere Valley. It's certainly cooler there, but perhaps the commercial pressures aren't so intense either, because these flavours are so piercing they make me shiver – with delight. Can something sizzle like ice? These flavours do. You can smell them on the other side of the room as soon as you twist off the screw-cap. Nettles, passionfruit, green peppers, coffee beans, lime zest and blackcurrant leaves – and all this aggression in a wine that feels as gentle as white melon flesh.

5 2007 Cabernet Sauvignon-Merlot, Moda, Joseph, Primo Estate, McLaren Vale, South Australia, 14.5% abv

🍷 AustralianWineCentre.co.uk, £19.99

Joe Grilli never lets me down. One of Australia's most original winemakers, his talent is made that much more exciting by his Italian heritage. Italian red wines often have a brusque bitterness and a mouthwatering sour streak to the ripe fruit – both very welcome in South Australia, where the relentless sunshine can produce soft, flabby flavours. Joe's having none of that. This remarkable red is a blend of 80% Cabernet and 20% Merlot – the classic Bordeaux blend. Not in Joe's hands. He dries the grapes after picking and before crushing – like they sometimes do in the Veneto in north-east Italy. The effect is shocking. The flavour starts out as though this is going to be a thick mug of tannic, leathery grape soup. But then the wine blossoms into something dense and fascinating and lovely. The freshness of blueberries and late summer blackberries binds itself into a richness of prunes and fig syrup and chocolate, while the invigorating sweet-sour acidity of plum skins resonates like piano wire and the tannin is as grippy yet affectionate as the lick of a cat's tongue.

6 2006 Tokara White, Stellenbosch, South Africa, 14% abv

🍷 Halifax Wine Co, Swig, Noel Young, c.£21

Quite possibly South Africa's greatest white wine. The beautiful, architecturally daring Tokara winery is really beginning to hit its straps. The white in particular is now making a glittering reputation for itself. 80% Sauvignon Blanc is blended with 20% Semillon into a hauntingly fragrant, dry yet full-bodied white, scented like Floris soap, fattened up with crunchy hazelnut and creamy custard, and scythed through by mouthwatering, crackling, snappy coffee bean and gooseberry acidity.

7 2003 Semillon, Allandale, Hunter Valley, New South Wales, Australia, 12% abv
♀ Oz Wines, £11.99

You just have to give these Hunter Valley Semillons a bit of aging. Tasted young this was sharp, citrus and zesty. It's over 6 years old now and is completely transformed, but these flavours are not mainstream, this isn't collar and tie wine. When you smell it, you think ooh, I don't like that, but then the sweaty smell develops into the lushness of homemade rice pudding and crème fraîche. Sweat, yes. Fresh, sweet, athletic sweat, the sweat of someone you fancy – that's beautiful, lip-smacking sweat. Mix that with buttered crusty toast and leather, greengage skins and lemon, and finish it off with more of that gorgeous crème fraîche. As I said, not collar and tie stuff.

8 2006 Carso, Vitovska, Vinja Barde, Parovel, Friuli, Italy, 13% abv
♀ Bat & Bottle, £17

Did I say the previous wine wasn't collar and tie stuff? I'm not sure this is even shirt and trousers stuff. But I think it's bizarre and brilliant – it comes from the Bat & Bottle wine company, and frankly most of their wines are bizarre and brilliant. You could probably take a pot-luck mixed case from their list and come out either a devotee or teetotal. But back to this wine. You smell athlete's sweat, fresh off the back of muscles still rippling from a 400-metre gallop. So you expect a beefy wine. You don't get it. The sweat turns to brazil nut, then apple crumble just before you put it in the oven. But you haven't put the wine in your mouth yet. What a transformation – strawberry and peach blossom, underripe Anjou pear, cherimoya (that rather yummy tropical fruit with perfumed, custardy flesh), an unexpected but delicious acid nip and an autumn toughness like the shrivelled skin of a medlar. Then I wrote the fruit was like a folk wedding of pink and white. Did I really...?

9 2007 Pinot Noir, Paddy Borthwick, Wairarapa, New Zealand, 14.5% abv
  ⓘ Armit, £15.75

New Zealand is putting down a pretty persuasive marker as being the next best place worldwide for Pinot Noir – after Burgundy, of course. But is it 'of course'? New Zealand and Burgundy Pinot Noirs are usually completely different. At the bottom end (though still hardly cheap) New Zealand sweeps the floor with the French. At the middle to top end, even if you don't take price into account, New Zealand does very well. And if you do compare price, well, pound for pound, the Kiwis have it again. This is a good example. It comes from Wairarapa, just north-east of Wellington. The Borthwick operation is only 10 years old, yet Borthwick makes a wine that positively oozes ripe strawberry scent as well as the wilder smells of leather cowboy's chaps and slightly bacony smoke. In the mouth, the rich fruit fans out in a syrupy warmth of homemade strawberry and plum jam, a hint of morello cherry, and its glyceriny texture is streaked with appetizing acidity and just daubed gently with oak. Interesting, serious, succulent Pinot Noir.

10 2006 Cornas, Brise Cailloux, Matthieu Barret/Domaine du Coulet, Rhône Valley, France, 13% abv
  ⓘ Justerini & Brooks. £19.54

Cornas is supposed to be the chunkiest, grumpiest, most beetle-browed of the northern Rhône's red wines. Someone should have told Domaine du Coulet, because they've made a disgracefully delicious wine. This is the most scented Cornas I have ever encountered, flights of pepper blossom and violet aromas rising from the glass. The taste is lush and rich, damson and blackberry mingling with the floral scent and almost brushing aside its slatey minerality and smoky, burnt cream nod to something more feral. Cornas is a suntrap, but this vineyard has clearly been bathed and caressed by the sun rather than blasted and bleached.

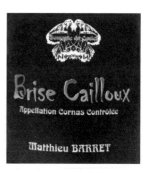

VOYAGER ESTATE
MARGARET RIVER

2004 | CABERNET SAUVIGNON
MERLOT

PRODUCT OF AUSTRALIA 750 ml

11   2004 Cabernet Sauvignon-Merlot, Voyager Estate, Margaret River, Western Australia, 14% abv
 Justerini & Brooks, £19.06

Margaret River in Western Australia is becoming more and more like Bordeaux. Well, I'll qualify that. It's becoming more and more like Bordeaux would wish to be, managing to blend thrillingly ripe yet cool fruit with a texture both gentle and austere that would bring tears to the eyes of a top winemaker in somewhere like Bordeaux's St-Julien. This Cabernet-Merlot is fantastically Bordeaux-like – yet actually most modern Bordeaux isn't like this (I wish it were). And although fine Bordeaux does develop beautiful fruit after 10–15 years aging, this is already at its peak, but could hold on for 10–15 years if required. With ease. For now, enjoy the brilliance of its deep blackcurrant and black plum fruit balanced against an inky, graphite dryness. Austere texture, yet with rich, ripe fruit, mouthwatering ripe acidity and grainy, pebbly tannins. Tasting this blind in 5–10 years, I'm sure I'd put it down as a £100 St-Julien from Bordeaux. Or would I? Dammit, if I were on good tasting form, I'd put it down as a 15-year-old Voyager Estate red.

12   2007 Pinot Noir, Cellar Selection, Villa Maria, Marlborough, New Zealand, 13.5% abv
 Booths, Majestic, £12.49, nzhouseofwine.co.uk, £12.99, Thresher, Wine Rack, £14.99 (3 for 2 £9.99)

This is where New Zealand scores in the Pinot Noir stakes. It's delicious. It's affordable. It's made in far larger quantities than any comparable red Burgundy. And it really does taste good. It isn't subtle, but its lack of subtlety is part of its beauty – even if that beauty is fleshy and a bit wide in the hips. The wine is rich, not jammy, dark rather than delicate, but the scent is delightful, the fruit full of black cherry and strawberry sweetness softened by oak. And the texture, well, I couldn't decide. Waxy, silky or the consistency of cashmere wool. Whichever it is, it coats your palate in pleasure.

13 2008 Chardonnay, M3, Shaw & Smith, Adelaide Hills, South Australia, 13.5% abv
♀ Bennetts, DeFINE, Liberty Wines, £19.99

Adelaide Hills is a coolish, wettish and beautiful (very) area of hills and dales, gullies, forests and sloping fields above the city of Adelaide. Adelaide generally bakes and is always short of water. A few hundred metres up in the hills, everything is green and verdant, with vineyards spread across clearings in the forest, cool and healthy. Australia's verdant patches are few and far between, and they teeter on a knife-edge, generally balanced between an unfriendly sea and a hostile desert. Shaw & Smith were among the first to recognize that the Adelaide Hills provided one of South Australia's few opportunities to make fine, scented whites, and this Chardonnay is very delicately done. It's full and round, the creaminess of rice pudding mixed with hazelnut, apple and peach, and the oak is pleasantly spicy, but in a mellow way, like the calm post-Lenten indulgence of a hot cross bun smeared with farm butter.

14 2006 Privada, Norton, Luján de Cuyo, Mendoza, Argentina, 14.5% abv
♀ Berkmann, Waitrose, £14.99

This used to be one of the great bargains in Argentine wine – full, generous and fruity and always selling for less than it should. Well, the price is now quite a bit higher, but the quality has gone up with it, so that we have a magnificent Argentine quality leader at a fair price. This blend of Malbec, Merlot and Cabernet Sauvignon is rich and modern, purple-red and scented with violets, marzipan and cloves. The fruit is dark and juicy, damsons and black plums toughened up with a little tannin. An affordable Argentine classic.

15 2006 Shiraz, Entity, John Duval Wines, Barossa Valley, South Australia, 14.5% abv
🍷 Halifax Wine Co, Liberty Wines, Swig, Noel Young and others, £20.99

At first I just couldn't work out whether I liked this wine or not. It's made by John Duval, who used to make Grange, Australia's most famous wine, and is dense and syrupy, with a texture almost of black treacle. Powerful, sturdy component parts have been artfully put together by Duval to create a wine in a casually rich, self-confidently lush style. But did it have heart? Well, I left the wine for an hour and came back to it. Transformed. Now it had a heart of truly delicious blackberry jam and chocolate and all the syrup had seamlessly melded with the tannin and fruit. I gave it an hour in the glass. Age this for 10–20 years and you'll be drinking one of Australia's new superstars.

16 2007 Pinot Gris, Te Mara, Central Otago, New Zealand, 13.5% abv
🍷 Justerini & Brooks, £11.83

Central Otago is New Zealand's most extreme vineyard, way down in the snowfields near Queenstown. Pinot Gris can be one of the world's blandest grapes. But put the two together and there'll be fireworks. After all, in France's Alsace, Pinot Gris makes great wine. This is Pinot Gris at its best – with sumptuous texture and weight – golden peach skins, cling peaches in syrup, crème fraîche with a light smearing of honey and the lightest sprinkling of salt. And through all this glistens mineral dust, like the blinding reflection of quartz in the fierce snowfields sun of south New Zealand.

17 2007 Semillon, Ghost Corner, David Nieuwoudt, Elim, South Africa, 13% abv
🍷 Stone, Vine & Sun, £13.95

Elim is potentially South Africa's most thrilling white wine region. It's a parched, squally landscape spreading down to Africa's southern tip on Cape Agulhas. Not enough water and too much wind make it a tough place to grow grapes, and there are only 142 hectares of vines. This Semillon is new to me, but it's pinging with personality. Elim gives an earthy, sappy quality to its wines, a nettly, leafy crispness born of the southern gales, but the Semillon fights back with a mellow orange-scented acidity, almost succulent apple and peach fruit and the gentlest of nutty oak.

18 **2005 Shiraz, Sanguine Estate, Heathcote, Victoria, Australia, 15.5% abv**
    ♥ Great Western Wine, £19.50

The soil at Heathcote is so red that even the sheep are crimson-coloured. But this is a starry piece of dirt. It's the oldest soil in Australia – pulverized red Cambrian rock 500 million years old – and it seems to have a remarkable effect on Shiraz. Such red soils often produce great results in Australia. This wine is dense, red-black, the fruit seems heavy as blood and is somehow juicy, stewy, jammy, syrupy, yummy yet tannic and serious and balanced all at the same time. More powerful than some Heathcote reds, but with the gorgeous, lush richness of fruit that marks Heathcote out as a vinous gold mine.

19 **2006 Minervois, Lo Cagarol, Domaine Tour Trencavel, Languedoc, France, 14.5% abv**
    ♥ The Real Wine Company, £15

If you decide to call your business The Real Wine Company, expect your customers to have high expectations. 'Real' wine implies passion, personality, men and women of the soil, proud of their produce. This wine doesn't disappoint. You need to swirl it in the glass, hold it in your mouth, and its full self-confident personality slowly reveals itself. It may start a little closed and tannic – but I don't mind tannin in a gutsy red. Wait, and gradually a floral scent starts to waft through the wine. Raisin richness is outmanoeuvred by black plums and damson skins. The perfumed rasp of peppercorn and thyme entwines the tannic bitterness and coaxes out an almost syrupy loganberry finish to the flavour. Real wine. You wanted it? Here it is.

20 2005 Shiraz, Bugalugs, Tim Smith, Barossa Valley, South Australia, 14.5% abv
    🍷 Oz Wines, £19.99

It's very encouraging to see some of these great Barossa beasts being bottled under screwcap. But this means the wine has been living in the bottle without oxygen. Oxygen helps to develop flavour and soften texture. So, a word in your shell-like. Don't just open and pour these screwcap behemoths. Decant them, or at least pour some into a glass and leave the bottle an hour or so. Let the wine breathe. It's an old-fashioned concept, but it works. This starts out powerful, dense, brooding – impressive but hardly a charmer. Come back in an hour. Suddenly the wine is richer, there's a scent of blackcurrant and rosehips and the blackcurrant is now really intense on your tongue and an unexpected, appetizing acidity cuts through the coating of black chocolate.

21 2006 Sojourn, Battely, Beechworth, Victoria, Australia, 16% abv
    🍷 Vin du Van, £26

Vin du Van's wine list is almost certainly the most interesting compilation in the universe. The trouble is it's not our universe. It may not even be a parallel one. When I decided to get a bit of background information on this wine from the list, I learnt to my surprise that the Dalai Lama is at present playing Norris 'One Hand Clapping' Cole in Coronation Street and is having trouble with his bunions. But anything about Beechworth, or who might have made this scary mammoth of a wine, or what the Durif grape is supposed to be like – not a whisper. Durif is a monster of a grape, but it does monster well. This is a vast, gloating, burble-brained hulk. I think it's dry, but it's so rich and dense and burnished brown in flavour that it may not be. Certainly the flavours of dates and raisins, sultanas and dried figs suggest it's a port. Perhaps it is. Perhaps it was made with a more courageous era in mind because this is here for the tasting of heroes of yore. In today's straitened times, you'll need to drink this in private, maybe even in the dark. Enjoy.

22 2007 Grüner Veltliner Smaragd, Erich Machherndl, Kollmitz, Wachau, Austria, 13.5% abv
♀ Great Western Wine, £12.50

Every year the Grüner Veltliner grape proves its versatility. The wines are sometimes dismissed as being light and scented with white pepper – what's wrong with that on a warm summer's evening? – but that's like saying Mozart is just noise. The Grüner Veltliner responds powerfully to its vineyard: Kollmitz is high and sloping, steepling down towards the Danube, and it produces a unique white. The texture is as soft as soufflé or île flottante, dotted with salted Devon butter; a touch of pepper and spritz break up this mild yeasty cake, and you realize there's a nip of bitterness in the wine, a bitterness like guava pips, or the pips of pears, which only underscores the smooth, cool fruit of slightly underripe pears and chilled white melon that make this such a high-quality glugger.

23 2008 Chenin Blanc (Unfiltered), Terroir Selection, Springfontein Estate, Walker Bay, South Africa, 13.5% abv
♀ Private Cellar, £11.95

Limestone isn't that easy to come by in South Africa, but way down in the south, around Stanford in the Walker Bay region, they do have a bit, and Springfontein makes the best of it. There's a lot of Chenin in South Africa, but too much of it is overcropped and underperforms. But plant it on limestone and keep the crop down and the results are magic. This unfiltered beauty is barrel-fermented to give it an almost Burgundian texture, but the flavour is modern Cape white at its best – bright apple blossom scent and boiled lemon acidity, honey and brioche warmth made just that bit exotic by pepper, allspice and coriander seed.

24 2007 Fié Gris, Vin de Pays du Val de Loire, Domaine de l'Aujardière, Loire Valley, France, 12% abv
♀ Lea and Sandeman, £13.95

I'm sure no one planned the flavour of this wine. I think its raw, rustic, knee-breeches and double-stitched smock personality has been evolving for generations – and God bless whoever decided not to interfere. Supposedly this is made from the rare Sauvignon Gris grape, but that's enough of facts. The wine sent me into a reverie – sappy, fresh-turned earth in a springtime farmer's field, the smell of sunrise, the smell of dew, the smell of mist lingering in the eaves of cottages clinging damply to the hillside. Old crab apples, kicked about the lanes by muddy boys, then harvested and stewed, the mud and the raw fruit finally finding some vestige of sweetness. Sap. Twigs, bent but not broken. Moist bark, fresh, green, and then here's a stem with that grey-green mould you find in dark, wet woods…

25 2007 Shiraz, Angel Gully, Joseph, Primo Estate, Clarendon, South Australia, 14.5% abv
♛ AustralianWineCentre.co.uk. £19.99

Joe Grilli, the hero of the baking plains north of Adelaide, also spends a considerable amount of time and effort south of the city in McLaren Vale. McLaren Vale Shiraz can be just a bit too much of a mouthful of stodge, but the Clarendon sub-region is a little higher, a little cooler. This is dense all right, seething with the dark lush delights of chocolate, prunes, blackberries and plums, black cherries too, and splattered with tar and burnt toffee and fire-dried herbs, but the hand of the master keeps it all brilliantly in balance.

26 La Guerrerie vin de table, Le Clos du Tue-Boeuf, France, 12.5% abv
🍷 Les Caves de Pyrene, £13.70

This is one of those inspired 'wines that time forgot'. I always look for such challenging delights in the Caves de Pyrene list. The grapes themselves aren't that out of the ordinary – Malbec and Gamay, banned by the local appellation of Cheverny – but by the time the Puzelat brothers have cast their organic spell over the brew something strange and brilliant emerges. If I had to work out what this really tasted of, it would take me all night, and my lasting impressions are of elements stewed, bruised, mismarried, bludgeoned and trampled upon. I realize this may leave you little the clearer, so I'll try again. Bark steeped in cider vinegar acid flailed against cold flagstones. Balsamic vinegar, raspberry vinegar and old rose petals soaking in a cast-iron cauldron. Cleansing, metallic tannin banging against sweet-sour rosehip and cranberry syrup, while the watching witches chew hazelnuts and hurl the husks as well as fistfuls of lovage and savory into the brew.

27 2005 Shiraz, Hahndorf Hill Winery, Adelaide Hills, South Australia, 14.5% abv
🍷 Nidderdale Fine Wines, £16.50

Barossa Valley and McLaren Vale so dominate the Shiraz world round Adelaide that you can easily forget that Shiraz doesn't have to grow in baking hot vineyards. To be honest, it's just as happy up in the cool wooded conditions of the hills. In fact, though you may lose a little heft, what you gain in freshness and minerality more than compensates. This is rich, but also very bright. It has good, dense, squashy, stewed plums and blackberries coursing through its veins, but the wine stays fresh. The smell of sweet cake spice has to argue the toss with the much drier scents of aromatic tree bark, cedar and polished leather, and the lush fruit texture has to endure the mis-shaven masculine attentions of some rough and ready minerality.

28 2007 Montsant, Acústic Vinyes Velles Nobles, Garnatxa-Samso, Acústic Celler, Catalunya, Spain, 14.5% abv
🍷 Lea and Sandeman, £12.95

This wine glugs out of the bottle like syrup, dark purple-red and lusting for a bust-up. Well, the first sniff is pretty rustic and out of order, but before you've even put the glass down the bearded giant has broken into a gap-toothed smile and opened his arms. The genius of Montsant is an ability to mix the sun-blasted with the fresh. Here you've got dates, dried figs and prunes on the rich side; cranberry, blackberry, rosehip and pink-fleshed apple on the fresh side; all bound together with a web of surprisingly friendly tannin.

29 2006 Cabernet Sauvignon, The Willows Vineyard, Barossa Valley, South Australia, 14% abv
🍷 AustralianWineCentre.co.uk, £11.99

You need to be a hedonist to appreciate The Willows reds – but that's no great hardship. The Willows always pack superhuman amounts of rich ripe fruit into their wines, but the reason I particularly go for this Cabernet is that they've found some lovely perfume and laid that over the rich, meaty fruit. This has a beautiful fresh aroma of mint, eucalyptus and violets as well as the more usual rasp of herbs to go with a big blast of blackcurrant richness, tree bark tannin and a burly chocolate aftertaste.

30 2007 Pecorino, Colli Aprutini, Fonte Cupa, Camillo Montori, Abruzzo, Italy, 14% abv
🍷 Bat & Bottle, £12.50

Suddenly there's Pecorino everywhere. Marks & Spencer has it; Thresher and Wine Rack have it; I even had it in a Chinese restaurant last weekend (went quite well with the prawn and chilli ginger dumplings). But when a wine comes from Bat & Bottle you know it'll taste totally different to any others. And it does. This isn't modern, pale, melony, herb-scented. It's golden, rich, awash with superripe goldengage and stewed peach fruit overlaid with leather and a rich bitter edge that grazes your gums and is somewhere between Bramley apple skin and lemon marmalade peel. The overall effect is of rich throatwarming fruit swirled about with tart, bitter peel and swathed in wax.

31 2007 Chardonnay, Ashbrook Estate, Margaret River, Western Australia, 14.5% abv
♀ Vin du Van, £15.95

A lot of people say that Western Australia's Margaret River is the nearest thing Australia's got to Bordeaux. Well, Chardonnay shines there too, and just when you say you're fed up with Chardonnay and you'll never drink it again, along comes this beauty. It's gentle, it's scented, it's fresh and crunchy yet still manages a suggestion of tropical fruit ripeness – and it has a whiff of that savoury sweat that comes so naturally to good white Burgundy. Dry, ripe peach and apple flesh matched by a little quince and pineapple chunk, scented with allspice and coriander seed, sharpened up with orange acidity. Lovely.
♀ The Ashbrook Estate Semillon is equally good – and cheaper (£12.95).

32 2006 Montlouis-sur-Loire, Le Volagré, Stéphane Cossais, Loire Valley, France, 13.5% abv
♀ Les Caves de Pyrene, £22.60

Another oddball delight from Caves de Pyrene. This time it's a Chenin from vines opposite the far better-known Vouvray. The domaine is a tiny 3 hectares and the vines are old and obsessively cultivated according to organic rules. Chenin always has acidity, it's how you wrap it with richness and spice that marks out the great from the good. The apple flavour in this is part loft apple and part the ripeness you get in an apple strudel. This opens up to a whole spice rack of ginger and cinnamon sprinkled into honey and butterscotch and fudge. The acidity mixes the mellowed taste of cooked Bramley apple peel with boiled lemons. And it's sort of dry, but with this richness and this acidity it's not always easy to tell.

BAROSSA AUSTRALIA
750ml

33   2005 The Baroness, Irvine, Barossa, South Australia, 14.5% abv

🍷 Playford Ros, £19.50

Why The Baroness? Maybe it's because the wine – from Merlot, Cabernet Franc and Cabernet Sauvignon – is a blend of burly Barossa and supposedly more 'feminine' Eden Valley fruit. The cool Eden Valley fruit has helped create a really interesting, almost atypical Barossa wine. You don't get much floral scent in the Barossa for a start, nor any leafy freshness (both very welcome here) but you do get deep, ripe, juicy blackcurrant fruit and liquorice and black chocolate richness – and they're equally welcome.

34   2007 Old Vine Carignan, Cuvée Christophe, Vin de Pays de l'Aude, Domaine de la Souterranne, Languedoc-Roussillon, France, 14% abv

🍷 The Oxford Wine Company, £11.50

The Oxford Wine Company has several wines from the Domaine de la Souterranne in deepest southern France, and they're all worth a look. This is my favourite, because it comes from 'old vine Carignan'. Carignan is one of the great ancient Mediterranean grape varieties but because it can be used to produce oceans of tasteless plonk, re-planting has been banned in most vaguely smart vineyard regions. But as the vines get old, the amount of fruit they produce diminishes and the flavour explodes into something quite unlike anything the trendier, more modern grapes can offer. This is a dark, rich, black fruit stew, almost syrupy in its consistency and tangled up with horsehair. Somehow some overbaked blackberry tarts have found their way into the mix, along with melted liquorice sticks, as has the shimmering heat of sunbaked stones. This is old-fashioned, palate-challenging and mouthwateringly good.

35 2006 Cabernet Sauvignon-Shiraz, The Scribbler, Yalumba, Barossa
Valley, South Australia, 14.5% abv
🍷 Flagship Wines, Nidderdale, Noel Young and others, £14.99

How kind of Yalumba to name such a nice wine after me. I can just see myself settling
down in the dark dead of winter, searching for inspiration, and finding it in a brimming jug
of this. Yalumba have done a really good job of maximizing Barossa Shiraz richness while
freshening up the flavour with Cabernet – that's the original Aussie red blend. This
wine has a fascinating initial flavour of blackcurrant and mint, scented with a few
drops of eucalyptus oil and a scrape of lemon zest. There's some decent rasping
tannin too and the whole experience is hugged by plump, chocolaty Shiraz.

36 2007 Maté vino da tavola, Sottimano, Italy, 13% abv
🍷 Les Caves de Pyrene, £12.40

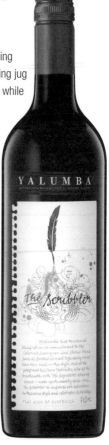

The home-brew of a distinguished Barbaresco grower, no grape variety, no place
name, no intimation of what to expect. Just quite a lot of money for a 'mere' Vino
da Tavola. Trust me. Off the record, it's the Bracchetto grape. Why it's in a
Barbaresco vineyard is why it's off the record. You only need to smell it to know
this is way off the beaten track – rose petals and Cooper's Oxford marmalade.
Corrupted youth, innocence degraded and decayed, the fresh petal brightness
of youth sodden with experience and worldly wisdom. Taste this dangerous
nectar. It's quite tannic – what a surprise – and the tannin has scent: dark
brown, austere, sluggish, like Assam tea leaves. Ah, but then back comes
the heady, flirty, petal sweetness, the bitter richness of Seville orange peel
and a faded rosehip scent. When I've swallowed it, I'm left with a bemused
memory of scented citrus bitterness overlaid with tea rose petal jam from the souk.

37 2004 Rioja Reserva, Contino, Spain, 14% abv
♥ Marks & Spencer, £22

I was in Rioja for the end of the harvest last year, and looking with some concern at the emergence of big, dense, brawny – and expensive – 'icon' styles of wine; made presumably, for the American market. I've always assumed that iconic status had to be earned, but many modern wine producers seem to think that if the alcohol level is high enough, the oak treatment excessive and the price astonishing enough, they can simply claim icon status for wines that didn't exist a few years ago. I disagree. But Contino – that's different. This is a single-vineyard wine, first made in 1974, and for three and a half decades Contino has been delighting the world with its subtle, sensuous elegant red wines. This latest release is from the superb 2004 vintage. It is scented with rosemary and pepper and perhaps a hint of eucalyptus. Its dry, rich red fruit is like syrup of red plums and cherries swirled around a hot tub made of wood bark. You know the oak flavours are there, but you barely notice them. What you do notice is the seamless beauty of the wine, and the fact that you drain the glass off with a contented smile on your face. I think that's worth iconic status.

38 2008 Semillon-Sauvignon Blanc, Brookwood Estate, Margaret River, Western Australia, 13% abv
♀ Oz Wines, £11.99

Semillon-Sauvignon started out as a classic white wine blend for top Bordeaux. Well, Margaret River in Western Australia has earned the right to claim that it also makes the classic style. This has dense, exciting, crunchy green fruit – and not from the usual green apple, green pepper and lime zest suspects. They're present, but so is Cos lettuce, and the sweet greenness of petits pois, gooseberries, greengages, fragrant lemons – I mean, you could go on adding to the list right to the bottom of the bottle. Well, why don't you? ♥ The 2007 Brookwood Cabernet Sauvignon (Oz Wines, £16.99) is also stunning – loganberry and raspberry, doughnut softness and graphite bite.

39 2007 Erbaluce di Caluso, La Rustìa, Orsolani, Piedmont, Italy, 12.5% abv
♀ Lay & Wheeler, £11.75

A lot of the white wine grapes in Italy don't have very much aroma or memorable personality. But there's a new breed of winemaker, a sort of 'New World' Italian, who looks at this unexploited resource with unbridled enthusiasm. New visions of flavour and up-to-the-minute techniques can draw out unimagined pleasures from the grapes. Interestingly, Orsolani has been making wine from the La Rustìa vineyard since 1894, and modernity and tradition produce a fascinating blend of flavours. The wine is as smooth as polished leather, like a new saddle just delivered to a renaissance notable. The sheen of nobility runs right through the wine – the fruit is mildest peach and pear, the acidity shy lemon, but there is a graphite coldness and the cleansing sensation of gunmetal before the first cartridge is fired. Brooding, imperious, waxy and polished, a memorable wine from an eminently forgettable grape variety.

40 2006 Montsant, Finca L'Argatà, Joan d'Anguera, Catalunya, Spain, 15% abv
♟ Laymont & Shaw, Tanners Wines, £16.60

Priorat is the top niche wine in Spain. There's not much of it made, and the price is eye-watering, but I suppose if you want to drink essence of sun-drenched rarity, Priorat's the wine for you. But if you want to drink marvellously balanced, deep, sun-bathed reds that warm your heart and leave your palate sated but inspired – for a fraction of the money – well, Montsant encircles Priorat. It's not famous, but frankly, I prefer the wines. I can't imagine wanting a wine more superripe than this – big, fat, dense, swimming in a syrup of strawberries and dates and dried fig paste and the burnt greasiness of baked aubergines. The tannin is positively granitic, but that's great – a wine this rich and dense without attractive tannins and fresh, shimmering acidity wouldn't be much fun to drink. And it would probably be called Priorat.

41   2007 Pinot Noir, Tobiano (Kingston Family Vineyards), San Antonio, Chile, 14.5% abv
🍷 Marks & Spencer, £16

Wow, this stuff is good. Chilean Pinot Noir was below the radar until less than a decade ago, when they began developing the chilly seaward vineyards of Leyda and San Antonio. Since then the quality of the best, cool-climate producers has exploded like a Guy Fawkes' fireball. This wine from the superb Kingston Family is wonderfully rich, full of cherry and red plum syrup. But its mad, marvellous, memorable personality is woven round its texture and its scent. The texture is of wax and polished leather. And the scent? My mind filled with wild thoughts of Russian spices and unguents, or musk carried on the soft warm fur of an ancient Russian trader to the East. Wouldn't you want your wine to smell so warm, so exotic, so animal?

42   2005 Semillon, Fox Hollow Single Vineyard (Tyrrell's), Hunter Valley, New South Wales, Australia, 11.5% abv
♀ Marks & Spencer, £18

They're asking £18 for this, and I'm saying it's worth it. The vines in this vineyard go back to 1865. Old vines give tiny yields of sublimely flavoured grapes, not necessarily dense, just beautifully balanced. This wine isn't dense; it's full, but it's fantastically dry, lemon and leather battling for your attention, lime juice spitting on to your palate. And then the wine simply transforms in a second on your palate. It's still dry, but as soft as custard and buttercream. The lime and lemon aren't gone, but they're now scents and seasonings in a wine that longs to coat your palate with butter and custard cream.

43   2007 Riesling Reserve, Trimbach, Alsace, France, 13% abv
♀ Waitrose, £13.99

Trimbach have always waved the flag for a haughty, austere, but crystalline and limpid style of Riesling, and when they're on song, theirs is the best in all Alsace. This isn't their top wine, but it shows the Trimbach style of restraint and clarity. It's bone dry, lean, still young, but hold the wine in your mouth for a while. Gradually the stony dryness dissolves towards mellowness, the steely acidity begins to throw off a citrus lemon scent, and deep in its dry, wing-collared Gladstonian core, a little honey and brioche stir. In 5–10 years time, the honey and pastry will match the metal and the stones.

44 2006 Crozes-Hermitage, Domaine des Grands Chemins, Delas, Rhône Valley, France, 12.5% abv
  🍷 Berkmann, £17.99

Delas have been making good Rhône wines for 20 years, but they're now concentrating on developing single-vineyard offerings, and immediately the excitement level leaps. Crozes-Hermitage has some superb vineyards and some dull ones; single-estate wines can be sublime. This is *not* a beefy wine. I'm not sure it's even fully ripe, but this gives an uplifting, mouthwatering quality to the floral scent and taste of classically smoky blackberry and cherry with a little hazelnut chocolate for company. Many current northern Rhône reds are flooded with loose-limbed, fat-lipped autumn fruits. With this, it's the memory of the first, nervous, wildly optimistic days of early summer.

45 2007 3 Amigos, McHenry Hohnen, Margaret River, Western Australia, 14.5% abv
  🍷 Wine Rack, £12.99 (3 for 2 £8.66)

David Hohnen used to make the super-trendy Cape Mentelle and Cloudy Bay wines, and his new company in Western Australia is already making waves. 3 Amigos stands for three grapes – Shiraz, Grenache and Mataro (aka Mourvèdre) – that are at the heart of France's Châteauneuf-du-Pape. But the flavours here are quite different – a lovely rich mix of lush red cherry and red plum swooshed with chocolate cream, yet brought to earth by a stony dryness and the gentle cooling brush of dried herbs.
🍷 The white version – Marsanne, Chardonnay, Roussanne – is good too (also £12.99).

46 2006 Fina Sangre, Haras de Pirque, Chile, 14.5% abv
🍷 Marks & Spencer, £15

This is an estate tucked into the Andean foothills. Despite having a most elegant racehorse stable as part of the property where silence and tranquillity seem to reign, the wines come from tough land and they're dark and opinionated in consequence. The wine is largely Cabernet Sauvignon and Carmenère, with just a splash of Syrah and it brilliantly treads the line between superripeness and overripeness. It's dense and weighty, but the blackcurrant fruit is sweet and delicious – despite the power, the wine exudes a fat, soft essence of superripe Chilean fruit leaving a few trails of smoke in the glass and a drying sense of stones and earth on the tongue. Power and beauty. That's the Andes.

47 2007 Monastrell, Cascabel, McLaren Vale, South Australia, 14.5% abv
🍷 Marks & Spencer, £15

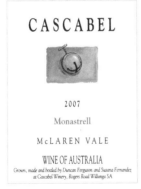

Inspirational stuff from an Aussie and a Spaniard in South Australia. McLaren Vale is a warm spot, whatever they say about cooling maritime breezes, and is ideally placed to try to lead a globally warming Australia away from French varieties towards Spanish, Portuguese and Italian grapes that cope better with the heat. This wine's 100% Monastrell – a grape used to having the bejasus scorched out of it inland from Alicante in Spain and surviving. Well, it positively prospers here. This is a remarkable, savage brew, sweet–sour, spice-laden, fragrant with cumin and lovage, scented with orange peel, thick with bruised plums and soggy cherries. It's as if someone has dumped some spiced vinegar into a fruit punch – rich, wild-eyed, excellent.

48 2005 Cabernet Sauvignon, Reserve, Edward's Block (St Supéry),
Napa Valley, California, USA, 14% abv
🍷 Laithwaites, £14.99

Napa wine is never cheap, and is often too dense and portly to be much fun. Laithwaites
have cunningly sourced this wine from a French-owned winery famed for elegant restraint – St Supéry. They've
done well. You get all the generosity and good humour of California without any of the excess. This is ripe but
not overripe, full of gentle, rich blueberry and black plum fruit, nestling in chocolate and sprinkled with cocoa
dust. There's a bit of tannin and acid to keep the flavours adult. If only more Napa wine was like this.

49 2006 Lirac, Roquedon, Alain Jaume, Rhône Valley, France, 15% abv
🍷 Lay & Wheeler, £13.75

Lirac is across the Rhône from Châteauneuf-du-Pape. The vineyards look much the same, but over the years the
wines have been relentlessly rocky and austere. Well, Alain Jaume has been making excellent Châteauneuf for
years and clearly Lirac was a challenge he couldn't ignore. Bravo M. Jaume. This is powerful but delicious. The
rocky arrogance of Lirac is still in evidence, but there's a heady floral scent and perfumed blackberry fruit where
nothing but sullenness existed before. There's pepper too, and the Lirac stones keep peeking through, but for once
they don't dominate. Perfume and rich ripe black fruits do.

50 2007 Chardonnay, Schug, Carneros, California, USA, 14% abv
🍷 Marks & Spencer, £16

Walter Schug has been making wine in California since Obama was a boy and has always tried to produce
restrained, delicate styles. He uses fruit from the cool Carneros region. He picks early, and puts less than a quarter
of the wine into vanilla-rich new oak barrels. The result is a wine that a Burgundian would be proud of: mellow,
nutty, lightly toasted, with ripe but subtle dry peach fruit and an oatmeal texture and aftertaste that is the hallmark
of good Meursault.

100 FOR AROUND A TENNER

When I sit back and think, what's the price range that most of my drinking falls into, it's this £6 to £10 or £11 range. This is where I get my New Zealand and South African Sauvignons, my Chilean Merlots and Carmenères, my Argentine Malbecs, my German Kabinetts and my southern French red and whites. It's where my Italian whites slot in, my Riojas, my Vinho Verdes…the list goes on and on. What isn't included here is much from the so-called classics: not much Bordeaux (though whites can be excellent below a tenner); virtually no red Burgundy (though you *can* find good whites from Chablis down to Mâcon). And in the New World you won't find much from the Napa Valley in California or the delights of Australia's Hunter Barossa and Yarra Valleys – in other words, wines whose price is dictated more by fashionable demand or historical importance don't figure. But the vast panoply of world wine does. This section offers the widest choice of styles and places, grape varieties and flavours. This section says – be brave, try something different. This section says – if you throw your prejudices out the window, you can actually drink better, for less. You just have to be open-minded enough to try.

- I've divided this section into whites followed by reds, kicking off with wines at the top end of this price bracket.

- Rosé wines have their own section on pages 102–107.

WHITE WINE

2008 Riesling, Opou Vineyard, Millton, Gisborne, New Zealand, 8.5% abv
Vintage Roots, £11.50

Millton made his name with organic Chenin in the warm but wet region of Gisborne.
This off-dry, low alcohol Riesling is another success – with soft lemon and apple fruit,
lemon meringue pie creaminess and an attractive savoury hint of cheesecloth.

2008 Pecorino, Colle dei Venti, Terre di Chieti IGT, Caldora, Abruzzo, Italy,
13.5% abv Wine Rack, £11.49 (3 for 2 £7.66)

One of the exciting new-wave whites that have raced out of Italy's leftfield in the past
few years. No one had ever heard of Pecorino just two or three years ago. But we
have now. I positively search it out if I want gentle but interesting tasty dry whites.
This has a lovely bright, fresh style – melon and greengage, apple peel, pear and
banana with just a little apple pip bitterness to make your mouth water even more.

2007 Pinot Blanc-Auxerrois, Albert Mann, Alsace, France, 12% abv
Les Caves de Pyrene, £11

Albert Mann wines always over-deliver. Especially when it comes to intensity and
spice, they always taste a rung or two up from what the label says. Pinot Blanc-
Auxerrois could indicate a pretty bland experience. Not with Mann at the helm. This
is a beguiling, slightly unsettling wine with a strange, savoury-edged confectioners'
cream butteriness, beeswax texture mirrored by polished leather and dripping
honeycomb and fruit that is somewhere between ripe apple core and grape nectar.

2007 Gewurztraminer, Réserve, Cave Vinicole à Hunawihr, Alsace, France, 13.5% abv
Bennetts, Flying Corkscrew, Liberty Wines and others, £10.99

Is this dry? Or not quite? When a wine is as lush and scented as this, it's difficult to tell – but then, another mouthful, and actually it doesn't matter. The sheer indulgence is what matters: right from the moment you open the bottle, a heavenly scent fills the room – Fry's Turkish Delight, rose petals and Nivea face cream. Or is it rose petal jam, or rose-scented talc? The wine keeps its vitality with a delightful acidity that is as delicate as lemon water sweetened with caster sugar, and a touch of brioche dough chubs it out just enough.

2008 Pouilly Fumé, Sainsbury's Taste the Difference (Domaine André & Edmond Figeat), Loire Valley, France, 12.5% abv
Sainsbury's, £10.98

Most Pouilly Fumé nowadays is a) too expensive, and b) doesn't taste of much. It certainly doesn't have the refreshing sharpness of Sauvignon. Well, this one does. It's got a bright apple blossom and blackcurrant leaf aroma, and plenty of ripe yet green fruit – green apples, green capsicum – and a whiff of coffee beans.

2003 Santenay, Domaine Claude Nouveau, Burgundy, France, 13.5% abv
Fingal-Rock, £10.97

I check out Fingal-Rock if I'm slavering after some of the wilder, funkier Burgundian experiences. Well, Santenay certainly isn't a mainstream source of white Burgundy, but this rare little gem is about as real as Burgundy can get. Lush, soft, but bone-dry texture carries a raft of flavours: coffee cream and hazelnut paste, log fire smoke, oatmeal, and that strange but irresistible flavour so many fine traditional Burgundies possess – sausagemeat, raw but fresh and made minutes ago by your local butcher. These quirks of flavour are what make traditional wines so special – and so difficult for the New World tyros to imitate.

2006 Chasselas Sans Soufre (organic, biodynamic), Pierre Frick, Alsace, France, 11% abv
Les Caves de Pyrene, £10.90

I look at this and think, no, it's gone. Surely. It's far too deep and golden. So I take a sniff and don't immediately change my mind – it smells like the apple juice you get in hotels frequented by ramblers in baggy shorts. But it's actually rather fine, rather weird and wonderful. The apple flavour runs right through the wine and there's a pale sweetness like honey bread soaked in apple juice or perhaps in Normandy cider, but there's a rocky, graphite core that makes it sort of tremendous in its strange way. Slate, graphite, leather, bay leaf, heather honey, all swamped by apple juice and cider. And it's under a crown cap. The label says this 'preserves intact the emotion contained in the bottle'. Bravo, Caves de Pyrene.

2007 Riesling, Bockgärten, trocken, Weinrieder, Niederösterreich, Austria, 13% abv
Waterloo Wine Co, £10.70

Very attractive, soft-centred Riesling. There is some acidity there, but it doesn't dominate the wine, it merely adds a green apple and greengage skin freshness. The softness is almost doughy, creamily yeasty, and is flecked with allspice; it might be too chubby were it not for a lingering taste of green angelica and greengage fruit and a dry undertow of minerals.

2007 Chardonnay, Chamonix, Franschhoek, South Africa, 13.5% abv
The Wine Society, £10.50

I wish the bottle were a bit lighter – if you're an eco-warrior, read no further; buy something else. But the wine is classy – gentle apple and peach fruit, mildly spiced with cinnamon and clove, a little syrupy richness, a little brazil nut flesh creaminess. Quite traditional, but none the worse for that.

2007 Godello, Valdeorras, Clasico, Viña Somoza, Galicia, Spain, 13.5% abv
Lay & Wheeler, £10.50

Godello is one of the jewels of north-west Spain. Albariño is the trendy Galician grape, but Godello deserves equal billing for its very different, much more lush and scented style. This is rich, indulgent, lazy-lipped, hedonists' white. Its flavour is almost bruised – like a lightly bruised apple or peach – and this actually helps its rather corrupt quality.

2005 Marsanne, Tahbilk, Central Victoria, Australia, 13.5% abv
Wine Rack, £10.49 (3 for 2 £6.99)

A magnificent throwback to a more hedonistic and self-confident Australia. This is the kind of wine that made Australia famous – ebullient, golden-coloured, bursting with flavour. It's made from the rare Marsanne grape by one of Australia's oldest wineries, Tahbilk. Marsanne is supposed to taste of honeysuckle: this is pure honeysuckle soaked in honey oozing from the comb. There's quince and golden-gage fruit there too, and a tasty stab of acidity like West Indian lime marmalade. A glorious snapshot of what Australia used to do so well – and clearly still can.

2007 Chardonnay, Chalkers Crossing, Tumbarumba, New South Wales, Australia, 14.5% abv
Cambridge Wine Merchant, Great Western Wines, Oz Wines, £9.99

Tumbarumba is in New South Wales. So it's hot, you'd say, Well, no, in New South Wales terms it's positively icy (i.e. on the cooler side of warm), hidden away in the Australian Alps. It's high up, and this gives this Chardie an insistent, mouthwatering acidity and a fruit skin chewiness which never let go their grip of the mild peach and apricot fruit and the gentle spice of the oak.

2007 Chardonnay, Wild Ferment, Errazuriz, Casablanca Valley, Chile, 13.5% abv
Co-op, £9.99, Majestic, £10.99

This Chardonnay never lets me down. Not only does it show the richness and intensity of Chilean fruit – here marked by gentle peach and honeyed pineapple ripeness attractively flecked with lemon acidity – it also consistently displays the texture and mellow flavours of fermentation in good oak barrels that you usually only find on a regular basis in Burgundy: hazelnut syrup and oatmeal softness. And it also has something very precious – a sense of place, a sense of where it comes from.

2007 Collioure, Cornet & Cie, Cave de l'Abbé Rous, Roussillon, France, 14% abv
Marks & Spencer, £9.99

I'm not sure I realized they even made a white Collioure. It comes from the savage land of dense, purple reds right down on the Spanish border. This is red wine drinker's white – wild, waxy, exotic, extravagant. The majority of the grapes are 50-year-old Grenache Blanc and Gris: they produce this remarkable marriage of apricot jam, fat apple flesh, walnut cake and stewed fresh figs that somehow stays the right side of cloying and even manages a whiff of blossom scent and the cleansing chewiness of grape and peach skins.

2008 Sauvignon Blanc, Cellar Selection, Villa Maria, Marlborough, New Zealand, 13% abv
Majestic, £9.99, nzhouseofwine.co.uk, Tesco, £10.19

Maybe in a tricky year like 2008 it is necessary to pay a bit more for top Kiwi Sauvignon. This doesn't seem completely dry, but that's off-set by lots of sharp green flavours with good dollops of gooseberries, lime zest and green capsicum.

2007 Sauvignon Blanc, Premières Côtes de Blaye, Chapelle de Tutiac, Cave des Hauts de Gironde, Bordeaux, France, 12.5% abv
Wine Rack, £9.99 (3 for 2 £6.66)

It's easy to forget that Sauvignon Blanc originated in the Loire Valley and Bordeaux in western France. But in Bordeaux you hardly ever see the grape name on the label, and the predominant clay soils don't impart especially attractive flavours. This wine comes from pale limestone soils, right up on the northern border with the Cognac region of Charentes. Sauvignon loves limestone, and with the help of a little oak barrel fermentation, this is an irresistible mixture of nectarine, coffee bean and chalky dryness fattened up with vanilla custard and toasted hazelnut from the oak barrels.

2008 Sauvignon Blanc, Soul of the South, Waipara Hills, Marlborough, New Zealand, 12.5% abv Wine Rack, £9.99 (3 for 2 £6.66)

The Waipara Hills lads haven't let the infuriatingly erratic 2008 vintage conditions get them down. There are good wines to be found in all vintages – you just have to search a bit harder. This Sauvignon has got good, aggressive, almost severe, green flavours, but I like them – green apple, capsicum, a bit of lime and the cold brush of pebbles.

• The 2008 Waipara Hills Chardonnay (13.5% abv) is also attractively lean and cool – it should be; Waipara is quite a marginal South Island region. Soft apple and nuts fill out into something more syrupy in the mouth and the gentle cream finish is pretty satisfying.

2008 Semillon, Tim Adams, Clare Valley, South Australia, 13% abv
AustralianWineCentre.co.uk, Tesco, £9.99

Tim Adams is one of Australia's greatest winemakers, one of Australian wine's nicest blokes, and one of the world's fairest producers when it comes to producing stunning wine and then asking a modest price for it. For this price, you simply can't find better quality in these islands. And if you've never tried Semillon, there's no better place to start than here. This is still young and has a classic Semillon flavour of vanilla custard and orange blossom with a nice acid zing. Over the next 10 years the custard will get creamier and richer, the orange blossom will go from mild mandarin to raging blood orange and the acid zing will get more intense and citrussy. As the custard turns to mellow fudge with age, the citrus grip will scythe through the richness as keenly and as gorgeously as ever.

2006 Soave Colli Scaligeri, Castelcerino, Filippi, Veneto, Italy, 12.5% abv
Raeburn Fine Wines, £9.99

You could buy a Soave for half this price, and at half this wine's age. It would be water-white, limp in texture and devoid of flavour. Or you could take a walk on the wild side with this and experience what happens when Soave goes the whole hog. This isn't typical – Raeburn don't do the safe and the predictable. But it is memorable – golden in colour, the perfume like a tired and faded blossom left forgotten on an orchard bough, the fruit like a dried-out Christmas loft apple you feel compelled to eat when you visit your spinster aunt. Add some leather, add some pastry, add some honey and a bit more apple peel and you can't complain it's not an intriguing drink.

2007 Sauvignon Blanc, Garuma Vineyard, Viña Leyda, Leyda Valley, Chile, 13.5% abv
Great Western Wine, Harvey Nichols and others, £9.50

This is smashing stuff. I took it along to a New Zealand Sauvignon seminar to show the Kiwis what the opposition is. There's 2007 and 2008 on the market. The 2007 is a little richer, but the 2008 is getting there, with a fantastic mix of gooseberry, green capsicum, lime zest, tomato leaves, beach pebbles, sarsaparilla and Cheddar cheesecloth. You think I'm joking? My next three tasting notes are panto dames, osmotic devices and Chanel No.5. None of which, in the cold light of day, can I explain. I don't even know what an osmotic device is.

2008 Falanghina, Biblos, Di Majo Norante, Molise, Italy, 13% abv
Oddbins, £9.49

For most of my wine life, Molise has just been a footnote in Italian wine – a 'nothing happens here, don't bother' kind of place. The revolution in Italian wine has changed all that. Di Majo Norante have always been good producers but now, by planting the fashionable Falanghina, they can demand to be noticed. What makes this so appetizing is the counterpoint between perfume and bitterness in what is a bone dry but lush wine. Scents of violet, apple blossom, mint leaf and dried thyme set you up for the soft, chubby peach and pear flesh fruit, but they don't prepare you for the fascinating bitterness of tamarind and almond skins, nor the glinting rock dust that trails through the wine.

2007 Chablis, Domaine La Vigne Blanche, Burgundy, France, 12% abv
Aldi, £8.99

Chablis is such a popular wine that every supermarket has to have one, if not several versions. But many of them pander to a kind of lowest common denominator and are just too soft and creamy. Why? Chablis is supposed to be chilly-eyed, haughty, bone dry. So well done, Aldi. This is bone dry. You can taste the chalk and the stones, you can feel the raw sharpness of lemon rind acidity. But you've got a mild oatmeal friendliness and a hint of honey to stop you thinking you don't dare take another mouthful.

2008 Colombard-Sauvignon Blanc, La Biondina, Primo Estate, McLaren Vale, South Australia, 12% abv
AustralianWineCentre.co.uk, £8.99

A brilliant marriage of opposites. My first impression is of a grapefruit and passionfruit zesty aggression, scented by lemon leaves, but immediately this sharpness is wooed and won over by a sweet-lipped, chubby texture of leather and glycerine and fluffy apple flesh, and the aggression fades to the gentle nip of citrus peel boiled with caster sugar. La Biondina has been excellent for years, and the 2008 vintage is the best yet.
• The red equivalent is 2007 Il Briccone, a Shiraz-Sangiovese blend (14% abv) – rich, powerful, throaty.

REICHSGRAF von KESSELSTATT

2004 SCHARZHOFBERGER
RIESLING KABINETT

2004 Riesling Kabinett, Scharzhofberger, Reichsgraf von Kesselstatt, Mosel, Germany, 8.5% abv
Co-op, £8.99

I'm delighted to find the Co-op offering this delectable class act – Kesselstatt is one of Germany's greatest estates and Kabinett is their most delicate style of wine. Scharzhofberg wines are as insubstantial as gossamer when they're young, but this is 5 years old and the gossamer has built up layers of texture and flavour – all soft, all mellow – custard and brioche dough, spring flower scent, white apple flesh coated with honey, a hint of petrol and the bright cool texture of the river rocks. Wine doesn't get much more delicate than this.

2008 Viognier, Anakena, Single Vineyard, Rapel Valley, Chile, 13% abv
Threshers, Wine Rack, £8.99 (3 for 2 £5.66)

Viognier is a grape that needs to be lush and exotic, needs a head-swirling scent and juicy golden taste to work. Yet it is extremely easy to overdo things and end up with a thick, sullen mouthful. Chile is proving to be an excellent place to grow Viognier and Anakena leads the way. This has a lovely, full, pear and apricot perfume. The taste is juicily indulgent, mixing apricot flesh with crème fraîche, yet keeping a lemon zest freshness and a furry quality halfway between a cat's tongue and apricot skin.

2008 Riesling, Waipara West, Waipara, New Zealand, 10% abv
Waterloo Wine Co, £8.95

Waipara West has always made good Riesling, sometimes searingly dry, sometimes in a delightfully subtle off-dry style that resembles a German Mosel Kabinett – and that's not easy to do. This is the off-dry version, deliciously drinkable and low in alcohol at 10% abv, with full, ripe, baked apple flesh, rubbed with stones, and sprinkled with lemon juice and kaffir lime leaves.

• The 2008 Waipara West unoaked Chardonnay (13% abv, £8.95) is also a delight – mouthwatering, crisp apple, pear and white peach fruit slightly mellowed by crystallized white sugar. I almost thought there was too much fruit – then I told myself not to be so silly.

2003 Rioja Reserva, Senorio de Laredo, Bodegas Laredo, Spain, 13% abv
Big Red Wine, £8.85

Big, rich, mature white Rioja: this is not mainstream. But I like it. The fruit is bruised and autumnal, the scent is of orange blossom and the texture is like custard mixed with crumbs of orange shortbread, or wax cut through with the juice of a blood orange.

2008 Vin de Savoie, L'Orangerie, Philippe & François Tiollier, Savoie, France, 11% abv Yapp Brothers, £8.50

Mountain wine – and it really tastes like it – with an uplifting aroma of fresh green apples just split open, anis and mint and hillside herbs and a bouquet of mountain flowers. The flavour is mild yet fresh as Alpine air, with a refreshing sense of ripe green apples and boiled lemon rind and a quartz-like gleam in its texture. Be original. Try this instead of Sauvignon.

2008 Chenin Blanc, Black Label, Esk Valley, Hawkes Bay, New Zealand, 14% abv
D Byrne, nzhouseofwine.co.uk, WoodWinters and others, £8.49

Fascinating stuff. In New Zealand Chenin Blanc is a minority player, swamped by Sauvignon, Chardonnay and now Pinot Gris. But when Esk Valley's Gordon Russell gets to grips with any grape, he always delivers something special. This is a bright, fresh white with mouthwatering, crisp apple flesh and lemon zest, dry thyme and angelica scent, wrapped in beeswax and honey. And it keeps changing in the glass – a mark of a top wine – rosehip appears, then guava, quince will appear if you wait. With its long, exhilarating aftertaste, this is excellent now and will age 10 years.

2008 Sauvignon, Touraine, Domaine Jacky Marteau, Loire Valley, France, 13.5% abv
Haynes Hanson & Clark, £8.20

Jacky Marteau is one of my favourite Sauvignon Blanc producers in the Loire Valley. Most Sancerre and Pouilly Fumé producers now overcharge for wines they seem to have wilfully de-flavoured. But Touraine is less well known and less popular – which lets Jacky Marteau offer more flavour for less money. This is bright, acidic in an attractive lemony way, with snappy green apple peel and coffee bean flavours and yet has a round, slightly chubby core to keep the acid in balance.

2007 Chardonnay Bourgogne, Jurassique, Jean-Marc Brocard, Burgundy, France, 12% abv
Booths, £7.99

Brocard is famous for his Chablis. But the Chablis region is pretty strictly regulated and there are lots of fine vineyards that don't get included within the boundaries. But they can claim the basic appellation of Bourgogne. This means they can't charge so much money for the wine. Light bulb moment. Top producer, top vineyard, lower price = bargain. This wine starts out a bit lean, but the flavour explodes as you roll the wine round your mouth – lemon pith acid spears through the palate dragging chalky minerals in its wake, while a richness of hazelnut and crème fraîche and an appetizingly savoury, fresh, athletic sweat build up by the second.

2007 Chardonnay, Fairleigh Estate (Wither Hills), Marlborough, New Zealand, 13.5% abv
Majestic, £7.99

Wither Hills is a pretty trendy label, so it's nice to find Majestic bringing in what is a kind of second label at a lower price. But there's no drop-off in flavour; this is absolutely the kind of Chardonnay New Zealand does so well – a lusher version of Burgundy – with hazelnut softness, apple and peach syrup richness and that slightly sweaty oatmeal flavour (the French call it 'sauvage') that marks out so many good Burgundies.

2006 Chardonnay, Limoux, Domaine Begude, Languedoc, France, 13.5% abv
Waitrose, £7.99

Domaine Begude is a lovely estate high in the cool Limoux, way above the fractious, sun-soaked bustle of the Aude Valley. Chardonnay is ideally suited to these hilly conditions and this wine has much of the elegance of Burgundy allied to the riper fruit of southern France. The soft white peach and fluffy apple fruit is almost chubby, but marries perfectly with the mildly perfumed oak and subtly evident lemon acidity. It's like Chablis with a smile.

2006 Chardonnay, Wild Mountain, Tamburlaine Wines, Orange, New South Wales, Australia, 14% abv
Booths, £7.99

This Chardie is called Wild Mountain – and they're not kidding. Orange is high up on the plateau of the Great Dividing Range, and Mount Canobolas has been known to get snow and sleet in midsummer. These chilly conditions explain the gentle texture and the bright, fresh fruit of this wine. Above all, the acidity. That's not something you get much of in New South Wales, but here it cuts cleanly through the ripe apple and goldengage fruit, the mild toffee softness and the wispy clove scent.

2007 Chardonnay, Yering Frog, Yering Station, Yarra Valley, Victoria, Australia, 12.5% abv
Majestic, £7.99

A lot of Australian winemakers try to make their Chardonnays taste like French Burgundy, without much luck. These guys make a pretty good stab at it. It helps that Yarra Valley has a fairly similar climate to Burgundy, and although the smell has just the merest whiff of the farmyard about it – very Burgundian – the wine itself is less rustic and more mainstream – attractive apple flesh fruit and ripe peel acidity, subtle nutty oak flavours, and the lovely oatmeal texture that is the mark of good Burgundy.

• Majestic also have a good, fresh, eucalyptus-scented 2006 Yering Frog Pinot Noir.

2008 Grüner Veltliner, Domäne Gobelsburg, Niederösterreich, Austria, 12.5% abv
Waitrose, £7.99

If you're tired of Sauvignon, fatigued by Chardonnay and are pining for a change, head for Austria. Grüner Veltliner is Austria's national white grape and makes a whole range of really interesting wine styles. I like it best slightly underripe like this one, because it remains attractively full-bodied, but throws together a gaggle of cool fruit flavours – pear, apple peel, lemon zest, white pepper – all streaked with chilly slate and granite and the freshness of long green shiny garden leaves.

2008 Pinot Grigio, Marlborough, New Zealand, 13% abv
Co-op, £7.99

Pinot Grigio, or Pinot Gris – the grape's the same – is New Zealand's new faddish white. Yet too many are dilute and hollow. This Pinot Grigio is the style New Zealand should be making. It's honeyed, it's got quite rich goldengage and English Golden Delicious apple fruit. It's also got a nip of grape-skin bitterness, nice acidity and a fleeting suggestion of grape-picker's sweat. That sounds like Alsace Pinot Gris to me. Exactly. Call it Pinot Grigio if you must, but make it like Alsace Pinot Gris and you might get somewhere.

2008 Riesling Kabinett, Ayler Kupp, Margarethenhof Weingut Weber, Mosel, Germany, 9.5% abv Majestic, £7.99

Lovers of fine German wines seem to be a threatened species in Britain. Yet Germany produces thrillingly different, delicate whites – and the best place to buy them at a bargain price is Majestic. This is delicate, low in alcohol, but packed with subtle flavours. Apple blossom, Cox's and Bramley apples, mixed with lemon zest and then boiled with sugar syrup and a little cool Highland honey. To this off-dry fruity delight, add a streak of slate austerity, and you have one of the world's great underappreciated wine styles.

2008 Riesling, Private Bin, Villa Maria, Marlborough, New Zealand, 12% abv Booths, Majestic, nzhouseofwine.co.uk, Waitrose, £7.99

Villa Maria is best known for its Sauvignon Blanc; the Riesling rather lives in its shadow. That's understandable – Sauvignon is fantastically trendy and New Zealand Sauvignon is a world-beater for flavour and style, while several other countries – Germany, Austria, Australia – claim the Riesling crown. Kiwi Riesling is worth a punt, though. This has an attractively not-quite-dry flavour of apple purée and orange zest and a scent of orange blossom. There's a good surge of acidity coursing through it, so you hardly notice its spoonful of residual sweetness, and merely appreciate its good, zesty style.

2008 Sauvignon Blanc, Alta Tierra, Founders' Series, Viña Falernia, Elqui Valley, Chile, 13.5% abv Laithwaites, £7.99

It's not often that a totally new wine region pops up and immediately wows everybody, but Chile seems to be able to come up with a new one every couple of years. This one is right next to the broiling Atacama desert, yet howling icy winds from the Pacific keep the vines cool and the flavours fresh. Perhaps the soft texture shows how close Elqui is to the desert, but the truly green flavours of gooseberry, lime zest, nettle and crisp capsicum make up for that.

2008 Sauvignon Blanc, M'hudi (Villiera Wines), Elgin, South Africa, 13% abv
Marks & Spencer, £7.99

South Africa is determined to battle with New Zealand for the Sauvignon Blanc crown. Well, it's heading in the right direction. This is exactly what a good, ripe, yet fresh Sauvignon should be.

There's a hint of spritz on the tongue, there's a fistful of green flavours – nettle, lime zest, green capsicum, cooking apples. There's fine-grained summer earth and an insistent acidity, yet the wine is balanced and soft.

2008 Sauvignon Blanc, Tawhiri, Yealands Estate, Marlborough, New Zealand, 13% abv
Co-op, £7.99

There's been a lot of amazingly poor New Zealand Sauvignon sloshing around from the 2008 vintage. Well, help is at hand, because the greatly superior 2009 vintage will shortly be on its way. Meanwhile, there is another white knight: Mr Yealands, who has planted a 1000ha vineyard in the super-cool Awatere zone of Marlborough. Awatere in general has produced 2008s far superior to the rest of Marlborough. This is surprisingly gentle, but packed with green flavours – passionfruit, Bramley apple, gooseberry, blackcurrant leaves and coffee beans. This is real Kiwi Sauvignon. Stick with the good guys. Kiwi quality will be back.

2008 Torrontes, Crios de Susana Balbo (Dominio del Plata), Salta, Argentina, 13.5% abv
Majestic, £7.99

The Torrontes is a local grape that thrives in the fierce sunlight, followed by a dramatic drop in temperature every nightfall, of some of the world's highest vineyards. These are great conditions to maximize freshness and perfume in a wine. This won't disappoint you. It's got a wonderful floral scent and a piercing citrus acidity that I put down as celestial loo-cleaner – but that's not fair. It's a really incisive lime zest, lime juice tang, in tandem with ripe grapefruit that cuts triumphantly through the waxy weight of the wine.

2005 Muscadet Sèvre et Maine sur lie, Cuvée des Ceps Centenaires, Château de Chasseloir, Chéreau Carré, Loire Valley, France, 12% abv
FromVineyardsDirect.com, £7.95

I'm not sure if a fad for aged Muscadet is ever likely to catch on, but Chéreau Carré are a law unto themselves, and this venerable Muscadet is rather good. It still has a slight spritz and a definite confectioners' cream softness from its time spent resting on its yeast lees (that's what 'sur lie' means). It's also got very attractive brioche crust depth and some nut softness and yet is bone dry and its acidity is positively minerally. Would I have preferred it younger? Would it prefer me younger?

2007 Sauvignon, Saint-Bris, Clotilde Davenne, Burgundy, France, 12.5% abv
FromVineyardsDirect.com, £7.95

This is the Loire Valley grape, Sauvignon, grown in Burgundy. For a long period the authorities wouldn't give it an appellation and it was like a delightful nettle-sharp itch on Burgundy's plump behind. Then they gave it a Burgundy appellation, Saint-Bris, and it became soft and well-behaved – sort of pointless. Well, thank goodness Clotilde Davenne still has a bit of attitude and actually seems to like the flavour of Sauvignon: this is full of squashy

green apple fruit, sharp leafy acidity, lemon zesty scent and a bitter apple pip nip. The acidity of the 2007 vintage has helped, but let's hope she keeps making this sharp-tongued style.

2008 Sauvignon Blanc, Los Nogales, Tesco Finest/Montes, Leyda Valley, Chile, 13.5% abv
Tesco, £7.60

I remember when the Montes winemaker Aurelio Montes showed me his first experimental Sauvignon from the foggy seaside slopes of Leyda. It was shockingly good. I'm delighted to see he's now making enough for Tesco to take it on, and it's still a feisty babble of green flavours – gooseberries and green capsicum, nettles and lettuce all underpinned by minerals and softened with a mildly syrupy texture.

2007 Muscadet Sèvre et Maine sur lie, André-Michel Brégeon, Loire Valley, France, 12% abv
Goedhuis & Co, £7.57

I wonder if it's time to rehabilitate Muscadet. Well, what should good Muscadet taste like? Don't expect an onslaught of flavours – that's not what Muscadet does. Expect subtlety, balance, a mellow gentle texture brought about by leaving the wine to rest in its creamy yeast lees (that's the 'sur lie' on the label). The fruit here is like the flesh of an English Golden Delicious, the acidity is mild lemon, the texture pale crème fraîche, and there's even a hint of honey and peach skin. It's like the pale sun slipping out from behind a grey cloud on a blustery spring day.

2008 Grecanico, IGT Sicilia, Terre di Giumara, Caruso & Minini, Sicily, Italy, 13% abv
Les Caves de Pyrene, £7.20

Caruso & Minini could almost be the top of the bill for a 1930s performance of *La Bohème*. A gargle or two of this could well help the high Cs, because it's exotic stuff. It has a sultry, waxy consistency and a yeasty fatness that goes well with the stewed green apple fruit. But then perfume takes over and coils of aroma open out in your brain – candlewax soon morphs into hippy scented candles, origami and kaftan. Is it incense? – no, not quite. Scented leather, yes, dry aromatic soaps, lavender even … and Jefferson Airplane. [who he? Ed]

2006 Semillon, Denman Vineyard, Tesco Finest, Hunter Valley, New South Wales, Australia, 10.5% abv
Tesco, £7.09

Year by year this is one of my favourite wines on the Tesco list. It's got a wild but brilliant flavour of smoked nuts, savoury custard, apple peel, lemon zest and petrol. And that's before you add in the disturbingly attractive sweaty cream and the dry rasp of hazelnut husks. This is serious wine at a very good price and it proves that if you want great flavours for less money, go for the styles that are currently out of fashion.

2007 Gewurztraminer, Sainsbury's Taste the Difference (Cave de Turckheim), Alsace, France, 13% abv
Sainsbury's, £6.98

One of the most consistently enjoyable wines on the high street. This comes from the large yet utterly reliable Turckheim co-op and, year on year, it has a beguiling, heady aroma of rose petals and Fry's Turkish Delight. It tastes of superripe grapes – not many wines do – and a dab of Nivea creme with a texture of waxy, scented, oriental leather.

RED WINE

2007 Syrah, Camplazens, Vin de Pays d'Oc, Château Camplazens, Languedoc-Roussillon, France, 13% abv Wine Rack, £12.99 (3 for 2 £8.66)

This wine, made by a Yorkshireman and his wife, has been one of the revelations of southern France over the past few years. Every competition the wine enters, it walks off with a gold, sometimes a trophy. Sea breezes and cool limestone soil produce fabulous fruit flavours – violet and blueberry scent followed up by what is thought of as the classic northern Rhône Syrah tastes of blackberry and blueberry, smoky cream, a bit of twiggy, sappy green freshness and some soft fudge from the oak barrels. You'd pay two or three times as much in the northern Rhône.

2005 Rioja Crianza, Graciano, Viña Ijalba, Spain, 13% abv
Vintage Roots, £11.75

Graciano is a rare beast in Rioja right now, since most of it has been pulled up to make way for trendier Tempranillo. But as the world warms up, Graciano's ability to keep its acidity in hot vintages is at last being appreciated. A single-variety Graciano is almost never made, so this is a great chance to see what it tastes like: it's quite rich, yet dry; dry strawberry and dark red plum fruit, plum skin tannin and a touch of tobacco and graphite to come. Not typical Rioja but good stuff.

2005 Sangiovese, Eldredge Vineyards, Clare Valley, South Australia, 14.5% abv AustralianWineCentre.co.uk, £11

As global warming starts to tear the stuffing out of Australia, they are going to have to turn to more warm-climate grape varieties if they don't all want to end up making

grape soup. Luckily quite a few South Australians are looking ahead. Sangiovese is the great Tuscan red grape, but here, under the open skies of Australia's Clare Valley, it ripens fully and exhibits fascinating depths quite unlike anything it produces in Italy. It still holds on to its grippy tannins, but displays stewed raspberry and liquorice depth, a strange, delightful, sugary yet vegetal taste like carrots Vichy, chewy bark texture and baked toffee warmth. These Mediterranean varieties could find a paradise Down Under.

2005 Rioja Crianza, Izadi, Spain, 13.5% abv Liberty, Villeneuve, WoodWinters, £10.99

This has the true Rioja flavour that so many modern versions lack. It is a bit weightier than of yore, but the flavour hasn't been compromised – there's still a lovely oatmeal and toasted hazelnut flakes warmth from oak barrel aging, ripe, slightly stewy strawberry and cherry fruit, and crème brûlée richness to round it off.

2007 St-Nicolas-de-Bourgueil, Les Graviers, Frédéric Mabileau, Loire Valley, France, 12% abv Corney & Barrow, £10.99

Find me a more utterly enjoyable red than this. It's bone dry, scented with the perfume of the meadow and riverbed, and as cheering as a May Day dawn. The perfume is sheer spring-flower optimism, the fruit is juicy just-plucked red fruit blended with raspberries into a coulis, and the dry texture is clean and spirited as bright glistening pebbles washed by the casual flow of a country stream.

2006 Shiraz, Tim Adams, Clare Valley, South Australia, 14.5% abv AustralianWineCentre.co.uk, Tesco, £10.99

Tim Adams' wines have such star quality, and his Shiraz has never been better than in 2006. While much of Australia seems hell-bent on baking the Shiraz grapes on the vine, then bashing the life out of them in the winery to create a pitch-dark soup, Tim prefers restraint, elegance and a sense of where he comes from.

In a world of behemoths this Shiraz is a delightful, twirling mix of eucalyptus and floral perfume. The texture is full, mellow, not aggressive, the flavours ambling between red plum and blueberry, mulberry perhaps, and a little rosehip syrup. This wine reflects the calm, modest satisfaction of Adams in his beloved Clare Valley homeland. Lush, balanced, reflective, generous wine. Just like the man. Well, forget the lush.

2006 Syrah, T.H, Undurraga, Maipo Valley, Chile, 14.5% abv
Portland, Stainton and others, £10.99

Undurraga is a sizeable concern. This is a special release of wine made from vineyards of less than 3 hectares. I expect more character than from their general releases – and I get it. This is a tasty mishmash of slightly rustic crème fraîche, a whiff of coal smoke and deep soft chocolate and nut syrup. There is fair fruit – blackberries – and quite mouthwatering acidity, but these are relatively warm vineyards, so although the fruit is not that focused, the wine will get richer and more chocolaty in 1–3 years' time.

2006 Syrah, Reserva, Viña Falernia, Elqui, Chile, 14% abv
Cambridge Wine Merchants, Great Western Wine and others, £10.95

Inspiring wine: wonderfully intense, wonderfully scented and ripe, but wonderfully cool in style. You simply can't get flavours as lovely as this in hot conditions. Chile is rapidly developing new vineyard areas and has an expanding and impressive roll-call of grape varieties at which she excels. Syrah is one of them. (Note that Chile generally uses the term Syrah rather than Shiraz, implying they make a more elegant, French-style wine.) Well, this is like a top northern Rhône Syrah from a *very* good year. It smells of fresh blackberries and summer evening bonfire smoke and then it billows out with a sumptuous texture – blackberries and loganberries, syrupy soft, but roughened by wood smoke and the lightest smack of tannin.

2008 Gamay Noir, Woodthorpe Vineyard, Te Mata Estate, Hawkes Bay, New Zealand, 12% abv
Halifax Wine Co, £10.95, Waitrose and others, £10.99

The Gamay is the grape of Beaujolais. It isn't grown much elsewhere and doesn't usually prosper when they do try it. But Te Mata, the oldest, grandest winery in New Zealand, clearly got a bit of a thirst for what the French call 'gouleyant' – gluggable red – and thought 'Beaujolais'. It's a triumph: bright banana, pear and strawberry fruit, some wood bark and sappy stems and acidity squeezed from ripe eating apples. This is a delight, just what Beaujolais should be – it's just I didn't expect to have to go 13,000 miles to find it.

2007 Côtes du Rhône Village Sablet, Domaine des Espiers, Rhône Valley, France, 14.5% abv
Stone, Vine & Sun, £10.75

2007 is such a good vintage in the Rhône. This wine from the little-known southern village of Sablet shows the genius of 2007: it's rich, dense, peppery, herby, powerful and yet it is *fresh*. All that dark, sweet fruit, all that grippy tannin, all that alcohol – and yet what is my final impression of the wine? Scented red plums, pink cherries, rosehips – all concentrated and intense, all amazingly fresh.

2006 Malbec Reserva, Jean Bousquet, Tupungato, Mendoza, Argentina, 14.5% abv
Vintage Roots, £10.75

I wasn't sure about this one when I first smelled it, but as soon as I took a mouthful I was hooked. The fruit is fantastic. It has a deep, lush, purple feel, rich purple leading to sweet blackberry and loganberry, swirled with spice and scattered with dried flowers. And it still manages to be refreshing. Tupungato is the coolest part of Mendoza: both Tupungato and Uco Valley are worth looking out for on the labels of Mendoza wines.

2005 Bourgueil, Le Pins, Domaine de la Lande, Loire Valley, France, 13% abv
Haynes Hanson & Clark, £10.45

Loire reds can be light and fragrant or they can be dense and dark, but they never lose their gorgeous drinkability even if, as in this case, you could age the wine for 20 years. Its power is a bit of an assault on the senses – that's 2005 for you – and the flavour doesn't seem quite finished. But it's magnificent, finished or not. It may still be a bit austere, but there's ripe raspberry fruit and raspberry sauce richness, buffeted by tree bark and scattered with meteorite dust. Give the wine time and blackcurrants will begin to glow in its heart as the raspberry turns to chocolate and the haunting stony dryness gleams ever brighter.

2006 Carmenère, Arboleda, Viña Seña, Colchagua Valley, Chile, 14.5% abv
Colchester Wine Co, The Real Wine Company, £9.99

Arboleda used to be tied up with a large Californian company and the wine was relentlessly disappointing. Now it's back in Chilean hands, and blooming. Using the Carmenère, Chile's flagship grape variety, this wine is rich and sensuous, a lush stew of blackberry and blackcurrant fruit, but with wisps of coal smoke and tarpaulin as well as the bitter-sweet flavour of the edges of a baking tin after you've baked a blackberry tart.

2006 Corbières, Domaine de Fontsèque (Gérard Bertrand), Languedoc, France, 14.5% abv
Marks & Spencer, £9.99

This wine is based on the much-maligned Carignan grape with help from a few others. Carignan may be a poor performer in some parts of France, but it's a star in the high mountain passes when the vines are mature. It gives an almost syrupy red fruit, rosehips mingled with red cherries and cranberries; it isn't too tannic, but it does carry a refreshing barb of acidity and a bunch of mountain herbs. You can feel the tannin, but more important, you can taste the mountain.

2005 Old Vines Grenache-Shiraz-Mourvèdre, Marananga Dam (Torbreck Vintners), Barossa Valley, South Australia, 14.5% abv
Marks & Spencer, £9.99

I know Dave Powell, the guy who makes this. No one has done more to seek out and save the little plots of ancient vines that sprout like tufts of facial whiskers right through the Barossa. These vines are 80 years old and they give a lush, syrupy red with a remarkable flavour of sweet strawberry syrup stirred in with the savoury richness of fried ripe tomatoes, warm earth and dried thyme.

2005 Médoc, Château Labadie, Bordeaux, France, 13.5% abv
Raeburn Fine Wines, £9.99

I don't find many Bordeaux I crave at under a tenner, and even this one is really a bit powerful for now unless you've roasted an ox to accompany it. But the quality is there – it's dark and serious and tannic – and 2005 is a magic vintage; if you can wait 6–10 years this will bloom with sweet cherry and raspberry richness, overpowering the rough tannins and the surly earth of the northern Médoc.

2006 Merlot-Cabernet Sauvignon-Malbec, Black Label, Esk Valley, Hawkes Bay, New Zealand, 14% abv
D Byrne, nzhouseofwine.co.uk, WoodWinters and others, £9.99

A blend of Bordeaux grapes that I would happily put up against any similar blend from Bordeaux – be the wine ten times the price – and I would back this beauty to come through. Above all, it has wonderful texture – brooding, serious, but with a hidden smile wreathed in the richness of plums and blackcurrant stewed with black treacle. It has an irresistible chewiness like the burnt black bits on the edge of a jam tart, damson skin acidity and a tannin as grainy as the pebbles on Napier beach.

2007 Merlot-Malbec, Gravel Pit Red, Wild Rock, Hawkes Bay, New Zealand, 14% abv
Waitrose, £9.99

Big, rich and oaky. The oak is good, although I think the wine could do with less. It's rich but gentle, full of dry red plums and cherries, and, backed up by fresh acid, the fruit outlasts the oak when you've swallowed the wine. Everything's dry here – dry fruit, dry oak, dry but soft tannins, but the balance makes it work.

2006 The Red Mullet, Pikes, Clare Valley, South Australia, 14.5% abv
Martinez Wines and others, £7.99, Wine Rack, £9.99 (3 for 2 £6.66)

The name isn't that inviting, but when you realize the producer's name is Pikes it makes more sense. This is a really interesting pair from the Clare Valley, sort of hoovering up grape varieties that don't quite fit elsewhere. I suspect each vintage may be different from the last depending on what varieties are available – but that's fine by me; I like a bit of unpredictability. The red is Shiraz, Grenache, Mourvèdre and Tempranillo and is a good, chunky red, packed with liquorice, blackcurrant and black chocolate and scented with eucalyptus.

• The White Mullet (12% abv) mixes Riesling, Viognier, Sauvignon and Chenin and comes up with a tasty dry mouthful – citrus, some metallic mineral and petrol (they may not sound much fun but they are classic flavours of Clare Riesling) and good lean lemon, lime and apricot fruit.

THE
RED MULLET
[by PIKES]

WINE OF AUSTRALIA
ALC. 14.5% BY VOL. – 750ML

CLARE VALLEY
Shiraz (68%) • Tempranillo (13%) • Grenache (11%) • Mourvedre (8%)

2007 Shiraz, Ebenezer & Seppeltsfield (St Hallett), Barossa Valley, South Australia, 14.5% abv
Marks & Spencer, £9.99

Good sourcing from M&S. Ebenezer and Seppeltsfield are two top vineyards, and these Shiraz vines are up to 80 years old. It's powerful, dense wine, chocolate-rich, nutty and coffee-scented with a sprawling liquorice blackness covering the red plum and cherry fruit. But it's remarkably well balanced for a big 'un.

2007 Shiraz, Max Reserva, Errazuriz, Aconcagua Valley, Chile, 14.5% abv
Majestic, Wimbledon Wine Cellars, £9.99, Thresher, Wine Rack, £11.99 (3 for 2 £7.99)

I've always liked Errazuriz, and the progress they've made in the past few years is thrilling. Here's an example. They were early into Shiraz in Chile. It was always big, powerful, but impossibly meaty in style. Now it's transformed. It's a beast, but a beautiful beast – as smoky as boy scouts' tarpaulin but as sweet as blackcurrant jam. This comes from a special vineyard and you can really sense the wine's place as black smoke curls up from the round mellow oak and the piercing brilliance of its ripe black fruit.

2007 Syrah, Vidal, Hawkes Bay, New Zealand, 14% abv
DeFine Food & Wine, Waitrose, nzhouseofwine.co.uk, £9.99

New Zealand thought it couldn't grow Syrah until a few years ago, but suddenly the Kiwis are world class at it. The secret is that Syrah is not that much of a warm-climate grape. It can do well in warm places –

Australian Shiraz proves that – but it can also make lovely wine in cool places so long as there's enough sun: patches of Switzerland grow tasty Syrah. Gimblett Gravels in Hawkes Bay near Napier is a deep, warm pebble bed with its own warm microclimate, where the grapes ripen beautifully, but they always retain a character of cool, of chilly nights and sea breezes. This is so scented, the aroma is like a newly-opened bottle of cherry brandy, and the cherry fruit flavour runs on through the wine – morello cherry jam, sweet damson jelly, the mouthwatering acidity of damson skins, some cool graphite and peppercorn and the oaky warmth of brown manila envelopes. Fascinating and delightful.

2006 Zweigelt, Altenriederer, Niederosterreich, Austria, 14% abv
Nick Dobson Wines, £9.95

Zweigelt is a smashing grape, but it's almost unheard of outside its native Austria. It's delicious and peppery when it's not quite ripe, but so long as you don't spoil it with too much oak, you can ripen it right up and keep its character. This is dark purple and the flavour is bursting with fruit and spice – cranberry, red cherry, raspberry and plum, with hints of ginger and allspice and a dryness of stones and wood bark that keeps the wine cool and northern, and leaves the impression of ripe red fruit grown in a forest glade.

2006 Marcillac, Cuvée Laïris, Jean-Luc Matha, South-West France, 12% abv
Les Caves de Pyrene, £9.50

Marcillac is one of those magical leftovers from the 19th century that should have perished with the local industry, but a few doughty souls simply wouldn't let it die. And here's why: a real wine packed with flavour and hidden valley personality at only 12% abv. It does smell a little rustic, but the true smell is of graphite and blackcurrant leaves and raspberry juice. It's only mid-weight on your palate, but that raspberry fruit is sheer, gentle delight, and it's brushed by scented lavender and the cool mountain aroma of ferns.

2006 Merlot, Private Bin, Villa Maria, Hawkes Bay, New Zealand, 13.5% abv
Waitrose, £9.49

In New Zealand's Hawkes Bay, Merlot is coming up with some rip-roaring flavours. This has the classic smell and flavour of plums and blackcurrants, some green leaf freshness and sponge-cakey softness. Add a little stony austerity and tannic toughness nipping at its flanks and this is spot-on Merlot. Then add depth and weight and you've got a really attractive, serious Merlot which could age 5–10 years.

2005 Cabernet Sauvignon-Shiraz, Hooley Dooley, Dowie Doole, McLaren Vale/Adelaide Hills, South Australia, 14.5% abv Armit, £9.45

Did I read this right? 'Hooley Dooley is an Australian expression of surprise and awe tinged with amazement.' I can just see those big, brash Aussies wandering about crying, 'Well, Hooley Dooley' at every turn in the road. The stuff they put on back labels. We should have a Bollox-ometer. Anyway, the wine's good – a clever mix of McLaren Vale heat and Adelaide Hills chill. The surprise and awe is how the flavours of liquorice and morello cherry, black chocolate and tar are brash and burly – a road-mender's cauldron of full-frontal Shiraz – but the overall experience is surprisingly restrained and finishes with a mellow, gentle flavour of Harrogate toffee and blackberry.

2005 Malbec, Nomade, Mendoza, Argentina, 14% abv Armit, £9.40

Really interesting stuff. Argentine Malbec from Mendoza can taste a bit samey – full and rich and beefy, but short on true personality. Well, this wine is made by a top winemaker from 70-year-old vines in the cool valley of Uco. The fruit is still dense and almost baked, its rough-cut acid a little coarse, but I don't mind that here – just have the steak ready on the barbecue. The oak richness is like warm drawn butter dashed with sour cream and the grippy tannin has a mineral edge like the Bakelite of old telephones. If you want to see its damson and cherry fruit at its best, decant it or pour it into a jug for an hour or two – and keep that sirloin at the ready.

2007 Malbec, Tilia, Bodegas Esmeralda, Mendoza, Argentina, 13.5% abv
Wine Rack, £8.99 (3 for 2 £5.99)

Classic Mendoza Malbec of the drink-me-quick variety. A lot of Argentine Malbecs are being made heavy and sodden with oak chunkiness at the moment. But this is perfumed, bright and refreshing. That doesn't mean it's not a big 'un – it is – but the violet perfume lifts your spirits and the characteristic Malbec *mélange* of damson, leather and a little metallic glint is sharpened up by good acidity and a green leafiness as crunchy as Cos lettuce.

2006 Merlot, Reserva, Carmen, Casablanca Valley, Chile, 14% abv
Co-op, £8.99

Carmen is the oldest wine company in Chile and yet was one of the first to modernize and begin to exploit the stunning intensity of Chilean fruit flavours. This is a proud, powerful Merlot (almost certainly abetted by the much more characterful local grape Carmenère). It flaunts its earthy rusticity and a vague veil of charcoal smoke, but gets away with it because the tremendous ripe blackcurrant fruit will not be denied, nor will the reviving acidity and the wild bitter-sweet aromas of liquorice and menthol that pervade the wine.

2007 Pinot Noir, Tesco Finest, Marlborough, New Zealand, 13.5% abv
Tesco, £8.99

Tesco's first attempts at an own-label Kiwi Pinot Noir were fairly ropey, but this is an enormous improvement. A delightful, direct style with easygoing strawberry fruit, gentle toasted hazelnut oak and a soothing syrupy texture. Very nice.

2006 Shiraz, Reserve, St Hallett Wines, Barossa, South Australia, 14.5% abv
Waitrose, £8.99

Good, traditional, beefy but warm-hearted Barossa Shiraz. Typically dense, rich, stewy blackcurrant and black plums, with some prune sweetness and a little leather. Hold it in your mouth a moment longer and the strange bitter-sweet flavour of liquorice starts to spread along with dark brown chewy Harrogate toffee. Add some bone-dry dusty earth and a dab of grainy tannin and you've got Barossa Shiraz in a nutshell.

2003 Rioja Reserva, Viña Mara, Tesco Finest/Baron de Ley, Spain, 13.5% abv
Tesco, £8.98

2003 wasn't an easy year in Rioja – like most of Europe it got so hot the grapes baked on the vine. But these producers are a smart bunch and managed to capture the ripeness but avoid the coarseness and produce a true, traditional Rioja style – bruised strawberries and souring cream with a slightly baked rice pudding softness and a little peppercorn bite. It's only the attractive Mediterranean overtone of sun-dried tomatoes and black olives that betrays how hot the vintage was.

2006 Cabernet Sauvignon, Antiguas Reservas, Cousiño-Macul, Maipo Valley, Chile, 14% abv
Tanners Wines, £8.95

For decades Cousiño-Macul were the biggest name in Chilean Cabernet. But their vineyards were right next to Santiago – one of their best old vineyards is now a supermarket car park. But they re-grouped, planted new vineyards and got themselves back on track. The thing I like is that they didn't just become one more modern winery. They kept to what is a pretty traditional style based on dense, deep blackcurrant, sturdy structure, and the swirl of coal smoke that used to mark out Cousiño-Macul in the old days.

2007 Côtes du Rhône, Le Pavillon, Château Beauchêne, Rhône Valley, France, 13.5% abv
Private Cellar, £8.25

The label tells me this is made by the Bernard family, who have been winemakers since 1794. A strange time to start, bang in the middle of the French revolution, but perhaps land was cheap – like, free – then. Anyway, they make nice wine. This has a very pleasant gentle strawberry and raspberry fruit just slightly bruised by the southern sun, but smoothed by soft brioche dough, then lightly scuffed by river valley stones.

2007 Pinotage, Beyers Truter/Tesco Finest, Stellenbosch, South Africa, 14.5% abv
Tesco, £8.24

Pinotage as a grape variety seems to arouse more heated debate than almost any other, but when it tastes like this, I can't see what all the fuss is about. This is delicious, very individual red wine, tasting of mulberries and loganberries, toasted marshmallows just singed by bonfire flames and kept serious with an undertow of tree bark and sun-warmed earth. It's different and it's very tasty.

2007 Merlot, Cuvée Guillaume, Vin de Pays de l'Aude, Domaine de la Souterranne, Languedoc-Roussillon, France, 14% abv
The Oxford Wine Company, £7.99

It does help when you've got a star New World winemaker involved if you want to hit the road running. Australian David Morrison specializes in maximizing the fruit flavours in the wines he makes, often in areas that didn't know the meaning of fruit before he arrived. Southern French Merlot can be dull, baked stuff but the only baked flavour here is the chewy bits at the edge of a raspberry jam tart. The rest is ripe raspberry fruit, refreshing acidity and a surprising waxy texture which makes the wine terribly easy to drink.

2008 Montepulciano d'Abruzzo, Gran Sasso, Abruzzo. Italy, 13% abv
Liberty Wines, Stainton, Valvona & Crolla, Noel Young and others, £7.99

The number of times I've been told what a lovely, scented, plummy grape the Montepulciano is, then I've tasted yet another crabby, ungenerous example – and mumbled, thanks for nothing. But this is the real thing, with fabulous pure dark fruit: damsons and blackberry, loganberry and black-blue plums. There's a scent of plum blossom too, and the wine keeps a little of its Italian macho street-cred with its streak of woodfire smoke, its plum-skinsy acid and a soft slap of tannin. Why can't more producers do it like this?

2005 Rioja Crianza, Monte Acuro, The Adnams Selection (Bodegas Medievo), Spain, 13% abv Adnams, £7.99

When I taste real Rioja, carefully, traditionally made, without any grand pretensions, I can look back almost as long as I've been drinking wine, because in the dark days when reds were thin and sour, Rioja was the opposite. Creamy, gentle, soft, squashy strawberry fruit swathed in vanilla, perhaps the bitter-sweet crack of cherry stones to provide just a hint of toughness. Well, here it is again: living memories of Rioja.

2007 Tempranillo, Wrattonbully Vineyards, Wrattonbully, South Australia, 13% abv Marks & Spencer, £7.99

Tempranillo is Spain's top grape, responsible for Rioja, Ribera del Duero and a lot else besides. But it is proving itself ideally suited to Australia. The classic Tempranillo strawberry fruit is in full flight, with a hint of liquorice bitter-sweetness, but Australia has left its mark with eucalyptus scent, and a seductively athletic sweaty savouriness. Herbs and limestone acidity are there too. This is a great example of how Australia must prepare to move on from the cool-climate French classic grapes to varieties from warmer climes.

2007 Negroamaro del Salento, Vittoria, Pichierri/Vinicola Savese, Puglia, Italy, 12.5% abv Bat & Bottle, £7.80

Rich, dense, rip-roaring medley of prune and date, sultana and syrup that somehow also holds on to a floral scent and refreshing acidity. This just sings of the warm South. Baritone rather than tenor, I admit, and if I'm honest this wine isn't the juvenile love interest; I see it rather more as an olive-skinned, moustachioed lothario of slightly mature years – rich, still effective but no longer quite fresh.

2007 Syrah-Grenache, Vin de Pays des Côtes de Thongue, Le Champ du Coq, Domaine La Croix Belle, Languedoc, France, 13% abv Stone, Vine & Sun, £7.75

I really like this because of its uncomplicated, fruit-led personality. It feels nice and rich and almost fat without losing its floral scent, its gentle red plum and rosehip fruit and its smoky leathery texture. Good, lush red from an excellent domaine.

2006 Merlot, Winemaker's Lot 198T, Peumo Vineyard, Concha y Toro, Rapel Valley, Chile, 14.5% abv The Wine Society, £7.25

A big company like Concha y Toro – Chile's biggest – often has parcels of very good wines that don't quite fit in to their main brands, or which are experimental or quirky. This Merlot (for which read Merlot-Carmenère) comes from the top-notch Peumo Vineyard and is powerful but sweet-natured. If the fruit weren't rich the swirling coal smoke aromas might be too much, but the black plum and blackcurrant fruit is easily strong and ripe enough to cope.

2007 Minervois, Le Rouge de l'Azerolle, Château Mirausse, Languedoc, France, 14% abv
Les Caves de Pyrene, £7.25

This is a delight. Vivid appealing red colour, a scent of lily stems and blue-black plums and a thirst-quenching juicy flavour of damsons and purple plums bulging with ripeness, which is intensified by appetizing acidity and the rough rub of hillside herbs and cracked peppercorns.

2006 Garnacha, Malena, Miguel Torres, Catalunya, Spain, 13.5% abv
Morrisons, £6.99

I've been a devotee of Miguel Torres ever since we met for the first time when I – and probably he – was in short trousers. Well, it seemed like it by the end of the evening. But I've frequently preferred his white wines – the difficult ones to make in hot Catalunya – and found his basic reds a bit stolid and dull. But this is more like it. It's packed full of the stewed strawberry jam fruit Garnacha gives, it's got the smack of herbs and it's got an attractive chewy bitterness like raspberry pips – and it's fresh.

2007 La Garrigue, Vin de Pays des Côtes de Thongue, Domaine Sainte Rose, Languedoc-Roussillon, France, 14% abv
Majestic, £6.99

Bright, fresh, spicy, scented red with a heady aroma of violets and cinnamon. The flavour has the gentle squashy fruit of red plums and apple purée but it's reasonably deep, and is livened up by herbs and the cool dry rub of pebbles.

2008 Pinot Noir Reserva, Nostros, Casablanca Valley, Chile, 14.5% abv
The Oxford Wine Company, £6.99

I'm delighted to see more and more juicy, scented, irresistible Pinot Noir coming out of Chile. Every year, more good Pinot Noir vineyards seem to spring up. Every year the wine is good. Every year it's affordable. This Pinot has gentle loganberry and black plum fruit, a lush, almost fat, texture – but it's beautifully balanced – and an exotic scent of eucalyptus.

2007 Costières de Nîmes, Cuvée Tradition, Mas Carlot, Rhône Valley, France, 14.5% abv
FromVineyardsDirect.com, £6.95

Costières de Nîmes is right on the southern end of the Rhône Valley, and its reds, whites and rosés all possess a vivid brilliance which is utterly more-ish. Here the fruit is juicy, vibrant blackberry and rosa plums, scented with lilies, spiced up with coriander seed and allspice and lightly nudged with tannin.

2005 The Society's Rioja Crianza (Bodegas Palacio), Spain, 13% abv
The Wine Society, £6.95

2005 is a lovely vintage in Rioja and will improve in bottle for years, but this already tastes fairly mature. Nothing wrong with that – easy, approachable mature flavours are among Rioja's greatest strengths. This has the typical charming balance between slightly bruised lightly cooked strawberries, mildly savoury pastry crust and cream and a little nip of pepper.

2007 Bonarda, Vicien, Catamarca, Argentina, 13.5% abv
Stone, Vine & Sun, £6.75

Hardly anyone has heard of Bonarda, but it's Argentina's second most planted wine grape variety, and in a hot place like this, its very late ripening pattern and high natural acidity make it ideal for glugging reds. But glug with caution, because it packs 13.5% alcohol. These grapes were grown in the northern region of Catamarca at 1500m (4930 feet) up. That gives you loads of daytime sun, but very cool nights – great for preserving fruit flavour and acidity. This is wonderfully juicy, with an almost syrupy strawberry flavour – sometimes I think it's that heavenly sweet-sour flavour of wild strawberries. There's a strong sense of stones and mineral dust too and when you've swallowed the wine, it leaves a really more-ish rich red fruit feel in your mouth.

2007 Grenache, Vin de Pays de Vaucluse, Domaine André Brunel, Rhône Valley, France, 13.5% abv
Armit, £6.70

André Brunel makes world-class Châteauneuf-du-Pape, selling round the globe for a lot of money. But he also has a patch of old Grenache vines just north of Châteauneuf-du-Pape which he can't include in his

top wine, so he sells it for a fraction of the price – to us. But the flavour is fantastic. It's fat, unctuous, scented in a way that's half medicinal, half orchard bower. It's bursting with ripe, syrupy cherry and loganberry fruit, has the zingy acidity that marks out the great 2007 vintage, and there's a little of that classic Châteauneuf-du-Pape smooth warm stone dryness peeking in and out of the frame. This is a steal that seems to taste more expensive every time I take a sip.

2004 Cabernet Sauvignon, Vin de Pays de Vaucluse, Domaine des Anges, Rhône Valley, France, 13.5% abv Big Red Wine Company, £6.50

Domaine des Anges is a delightful estate started by an Englishman back in the 1970s which showed the locals how good their traditional Côtes du Ventoux wines could be if they only made a bit more effort. Well, Cabernet Sauvignon is very untraditional in this area, but the results are delicious – and you can really get a sense of sun-bleached hillside stones, and pine resin and wild thyme swept into the vineyard by the howling Mistral. Add delightful blackberry and plum fruit and this is a class act at a very fair price.

2007 Marselan, Vin de Pays d'Oc, Domaine de la Ferrandière, Languedoc-Roussillon, France, 13.5% abv Waterloo Wine Co, £6.25

Marselan is a fairly new grape variety that should not be approached by those of a nervous disposition – yes, there are scientists whose sole job is to create new grape varieties; as if we didn't have enough already. This is a massive beast. I suspect they'd had a works outing to Frankenstein's lab before nailing Marselan: unsubtle, thick – but good thick! – stewed, dense, hard tannin and acidity mixed with sultanas and dates, freshened up by raspberries and plums. Somehow it doesn't get out of control and ends up as a top midwinter red.

2006 Valpolicella Ripasso, Asda Extra Special, Veneto, Italy, 13% abv Asda, £6.14

Don't let the name Valpolicella steer you into thinking that this is thin, forgettable pap. Firstly, Valpolicella is nowadays making some delightful light reds, full of scent and juicy fruit. Secondly, check out that word 'Ripasso' on the label. Ripasso means the wine has sort of undergone two fermentations – it's complicated – but this greatly increases the rich flavours of the wine and gives it a wild edge. This almost smells of perfumed candles, and has a fascinating sweet-sour style with dollops of stewy cherry and strawberry soaked in a slightly sour syrup and bashed with just a bit of chewy tannin.

AROUND £5

With the chaos of a collapsed pound, a government hell bent on taxing the living daylights out of wine drinkers, supermarkets determined to preserve price points and yet equally determined to maximize profits, and poor old independent wine merchants without big financial resources and MPs' expenses to fall back on simply trying to stay afloat, the area of the five quid bottle of wine is a minefield. A fiver a bottle is top whack for a lot of wine drinkers, and it's definitely an aspirational price point to trade up to for many others. It's one of our most important categories – wine for a fiver. That's the reason why a lot of £4.99 wines are no longer as good as they used to be. Supermarkets refuse to pay producers more, even though production costs, currency fluctuations and government taxation all add to the real cost of wine. Often the only choice is for producers to cheapen and dilute the wine in the bottle. Well, you won't find such wines here. There is a welter of wines that can be sold at about a fiver with profit available to all, and pleasure guaranteed for us drinkers. Even so, I'm keenly aware that independent merchants in particular simply can't go on absorbing costs. So I've decided that if the wine is nearer £6 than £5 but it's worth it – in it goes.

• In this section you will find white wines first, then reds, in descending price order.

WHITE WINE

2008 Vinho Verde, Quinta de Azevedo (Sogrape), Portugal, 10.5% abv
Majestic, £6.24, Waitrose, £5.99

This seems to get better with every vintage. If you're tired of Sauvignon, but want your wine unoaked and bone dry, you must try this. Pale, quite full bodied, slightly prickly on the tongue, with underripe white peach and apple flesh fruit scoured by pebbles, rubbed with tobacco and subtly speared by lemon acidity.

2008 Chenin Blanc (cool-fermented), La Grille, Loire Valley, France, 11% abv
Majestic, £5.99

Underripe Chenin can be a pretty lip-puckering experience, but this example – only 11% alcohol – really works. It doesn't taste raw at all, merely fresh and thirst-quenching. It has a slight prickle to it, very pleasant, almost insubstantial, nebulous fluffy apple fruit and a real sense of the soft, moist chalk that Chenin loves to grow on when it gets the chance.

2007 Sauvignon Blanc-Verdejo, Storks' Tower, Hijos de Antonio Barcelo, Vino de la Tierra de Castilla y León, Spain, 12.5% abv
Tesco, £5.99

It seems unlikely that such an arid, stony region as Castille could come up with such fresh bright whites. But that's the particular magic of the local Verdejo grape, and when you mix it in with Sauvignon you can get even more

fruit. This has a gentle flavour of apple and honey and a little lemon and custard.
It has a waxy feel, a hint of peppery dust, and just enough acidity to keep it refreshing.

2008 Soave Classico, Terre di Monteforte, Cantina di Monteforte, Veneto, Italy, 12.5% abv
Hicks & Don, Hedley Wright, Liberty Wines and others, £5.99

Soave's got a bad name because of oceans of tasteless swill sent over here for
us to drink at parties when there's nothing else left. But proper Soave from decent
vineyards (Classico means it comes from the decent vineyards) is a really nice
drink – soft, waxy, velvety even, mild pear and apple fruit, a sprinkling of high
summer dust, a hint of leather cushion in a tented village, everything mild,
cool in a warm world, a shaded view over an azure lake… Now look what
you've started. It's nice wine, though.

2008 Fiano, Asda Extra Special (Cantine Settesoli), Sicily, Italy, 13% abv
Asda, £5.97

There's a wave of Italian white varieties hitting our shelves that should delight
those of us who are fed up with oaky whites, but find Sauvignon just a bit too
tasty. The Italian whites are generally soft, clean, dry, with mild fruit and herb
scents and flavours. Not earth-shattering, but very attractive. This is a case in
point. Top-quality Sicilian winemaking has produced a delightful wine – full-
flavoured, but dry, a flavour of baked pears and banana, a little thyme and
lavender scent plus good lemon flower and lemon pith acidity and bite.

• Tesco's own-label Fiano (£5.99) is made by the same producer in Sicily.

2008 The Society's Chilean Chardonnay (Concha y Toro), Casablanca Valley, Chile, 13.5% abv
The Wine Society, £5.75

This new vintage is a complete change – for the better. I used to think the Society's Chardonnay was very pleasant but altogether rather stolid – I felt I'd need to be wearing a tweed jacket and brogues and sunk in an old leather armchair to get the best out of it. But good grief, this is modern. Harumph. Fresh apple, a shred of lemon and grapefruit zest, nutty oak and soothing yeasty cream. Make mine a double. Pip pip!

2007 Macabeu-Chardonnay, Conca de Barberà, Castillo de Montblanc, Catalunya, Spain, 13% abv
Christopher Piper, £5.70

The name says it all – Castillo de Montblanc, castle of the white mountain, the pale limestone soils. There aren't many places cool enough to grow fresh whites in Catalunya, but Conca de Barberà is high and cool, and it does have limestone. This blend of Macabeu and Chardonnay has fresh, soft, apple-core fruit and lemon-curd creaminess streaked with lemon and a little mint leaf. Modern Spain at its best.

2008 Vin de Pays du Gers, Lesc, Producteurs Plaimont, South-West France, 11.5% abv
Les Caves de Pyrene, £5.40

Plaimont is a big, serious, quality-oriented producer in the Armagnac country of South-West France. It's particularly good at affordable, snappy whites, and good wine merchants such as Caves de Pyrene go down and blend their own cuvées. This is a delightful fresh white – easy, green apple flesh with lemon peel scent and lemon juice acid and a sprig or two of anise.

2008 Verdicchio dei Castelli di Jesi, Moncaro, Marche, Italy, 12.5% abv
Waitrose, £4.99

Verdicchio is another of Italy's white grapes that is now beginning to make a name for itself on the Adriatic coast. Actually, good Verdicchio has been quietly appreciated in Italy for a long time, but most of the stuff exported was pretty drab stuff. This is much better: full, soft, almost waxy, with ripe, spicy, fluffy apple flesh – almost as though someone had stuck a clove in the apple and sprinkled cinnamon on top – and a slight almond bitterness that works very well.

RED WINE

2008 Bardolino, Recchia, Veneto, Italy, 12.5% abv
Waitrose, £5.99

What a delightful mouthful of simplicity. Bardolino is a light red utterly without complexity whose only intention is to please and refresh. Most of it's drunk by the shores of Lake Garda, so imagine yourself there as you gulp this mouthwateringly easygoing sweet-sour mix of cherry and pink apple spiced up just a touch with sage and peppercorn.

2007 Côtes du Rhône Villages, Sainsbury's Taste the Difference (M Chapoutier), Rhône Valley, France, 14.5% abv
Sainsbury's, £5.99

Someone must have put something in Michel Chapoutier's breakfast tisane during the 2007 vintage. His expensive wines have always been good, but in 2007 his basics excelled themselves. This is really serious Côtes du Rhône – rich loganberry and strawberry fruit, deepened by sloes and rosehip syrup, freshened by herbs and toughened with bitter bark tannin. Add to that 2007's piercingly pure acidity and this is worth several pounds more. Oz's tip: decant it for 2 hours before you drink it to maximize its fruit and scent.

2007 Merlot, Miramonte Ridge Red (Viña Casablanca), Rapel Valley, Chile, 13.5% abv
Morrisons, £5.99

In a changing world, thank heaven Chilean reds keep on doing what they're so good at – offering great value and great flavour. Sometimes the fruit is dense and black, sometimes it's juicier and red. This is on the red side – rich, ripe red cherry and strawberry fruit that manages to be lush yet a bit savoury at the same time – with appetizing tannin and acidity, and the merest suggestion of coal smoke that lingers in the glass.

2007 Merlot, Sainsbury's Taste the Difference (Viña Errázuriz), Curicó, Chile, 14% abv Sainsbury's, £5.99

Beefy, burly, old-style Chilean Merlot. Up until about 10 years ago, most Chilean 'Merlot' was actually made from the dark-hearted, thrilling Carmenère grape. Well, I reckon there's still a fair amount of Carmenère in this, because it's rich and dense, packed with blackcurrant and black plum fruit, coiled in coal smoke and seasoned with fresh ground peppercorns. That's Carmenère style, and this Merlot is all the better for it.

2008 Nero d'Avola, Tesco Finest (Cantine Settesoli), Sicily, Italy, 13.5% abv Tesco, £5.99

Sicily is proving itself to be one of Italy's best wine regions – for all types and colours of wine. A generation ago – hey, less – almost nothing of any quality came out of Sicily except for the odd bottle of Marsala. What a transformation. Partly it's because of investment and a bunch of very committed wine people. Partly it's the realization that Sicily's own grape varieties are brimming full of character. Nero d'Avola is rapidly attaining world status. See why by starting with this example – full, rich, juicy blackberry and morello cherry fruit, gentle cream texture, mild kitchen spice to add allure and a new banana freshness.

2008 Tannat, El Esteco (Michel Torino), Calchaquí Valley, Argentina, 13.5% abv Marks & Spencer, £5.99

Tannat is a tough old grape, grown in South-West France and Uruguay largely because it is resistant to damp and disease, not because it often ripens satisfactorily. Has it at last found its perfect resting place in the vertiginously high Andean vineyards of northern Argentina, where rot isn't a problem, the sun shines fiercely every day and the temperature plummets every night, encouraging intense colour and whatever scent the grape possesses? What about violet, or lily? Yes! The colour is dark purple, the tannin is marked, but it has a thick-lipped, exotic red fruit, heady scent, a bit more oak than it needs, and a vivid character that makes this is a seriously fascinating wine.

2008 Chilean Cabernet Sauvignon, Asda Extra Special, Aconcagua Valley, Chile, 13.5% abv Asda, £5.98

Chile is just so good at this price point for big, juicy, serious yet sexy red wines. Tons of fruit and personality, good acidity and tannin to make them ideal for a meal. This one's packed with dark cherry and plum flesh fruit, a fresh acidity like red plum skins, and a lush fruit syrup finish. And this is a dry red I'm talking about. That's the genius of Chile.

2008 Merlot, Rio Alto Classic, Viña San Esteban, Aconcagua Valley, Chile, 13.5% abv
The Oxford Wine Company, £5.95

Rich, dark red plum and raisin stew. This is excellent chunky, chewy red. You get some real sense of ripeness through that slight raisin taste, but the basic flavour is big, broad, plummy and fresh.

• They also do a Shiraz (also £5.95) which is a gentle, blackberryish red that reminds me ever so vaguely of my first school camping trips under tarpaulin. No, please, no details.

2007 The Society's Australian Spicy Red (Bleasdale Winery), Langhorne Creek, South Australia, 14% abv
The Wine Society, £5.75

Bleasdale Winery, where this is made, doesn't seem to have changed since William Gladstone was in short trousers, and the Potts family who run it have been there pretty much since South Australia was settled. Is that a good or a bad thing? When it comes to making your Shiraz proper and spicy, I suspect it's a good thing. Nothing fancy, just do what it says on the bottle. And this delivers. Deep raspberry and black plum fruit, with fresh acidity, kitchen spice sprinkled all over the place, a bit of eucalyptus scent from the gum trees near the vineyard, and a dash of rosehip for the ladies. Hmm. I like rosehip.

2007 Grenache Noir, La Différence, Vin de Pays des Côtes Catalanes, Languedoc-Roussillon, France, 14.5% abv Morrisons, £5.69

The excellent La Différence's take on Grenache from France's far south. Absolutely classic flavours of rich, sun-soaked grapes – and the Grenache really likes to soak up the sun. It's gutsy, serious, quite tannic and chewy but with heaps of sweet strawberry and mulberry fruit and a big fistful of hillside herbs.

NV The Society's French Full Red, Vin de Pays des Côtes Catalanes, Languedoc-Roussillon, France, 13.5% abv
The Wine Society, £5.50

They don't mess about, those boys at the Wine Society. They say French Full Red – they mean it. This comes from France's far south, just before the Pyrenees. Wines can get pretty baked and wind-parched down there, but this is a delicious, mouthfilling yet fresh-spirited mix of loganberries and rosehips, bayleaf and basil and the mildest thud of mountain rock – after all, it is French Full Red.

2008 Garnacha, Vineyard X (Bodegas Borsao), Campo de Borja, Spain, 13.5% abv
Threshers, Wine Rack, £5.49 (3 for 2 £3.66)

Fabulous party red. At most parties, you have a couple of glasses of the cheap red and then furtively look about to see if anyone's making cocktails, or chilling alcopops, or chugging cider... anything, really, but not another glass of gut rot. Well, all partygoers should load up on this. It's the juiciest, spiciest, riproaringest loganberry, raspberry, strawberry, herb paste and the odd rock thrown in fruit bomb you'll find anywhere on the high street.

2007 Grenache-Syrah-Mourvèdre, Vin de Pays d'Oc, Domaine La Croix Martelle, Languedoc-Roussillon, France, 14% abv
Waitrose, £5.49

The vast area covered by Vin de Pays d'Oc may contain some pretty dull grog, but when an estate sets out to excel, you can find brilliant flavours for far less money than they deserve to get. This is made from the same grapes as the really pricey Châteauneuf-du-Pape. They're organically grown, and the producers clearly have Châteauneuf in their sights – but only charge a fraction of the price. Really interesting, rich stuff. Strawberry sauce fruit that fills out into blackberry and plum, very precise acidity and tannin and crunchy peppercorn and hillside herbs.

2007 Carignan, La Différence, Vin de Pays des Côtes Catalanes, Languedoc-Roussillon, France, 14% abv
Asda, Co-op, Tesco, £4.99

La Différence is a brand with a difference. For a start it's usually on sale at full price in the supermarkets, so the wine in the bottle is worth the price you pay. Secondly, the grape varieties it chooses and the regions it sources the wines from are rarely popular or renowned, so there's no price inflation. This Carignan is the supreme example. No one wants Carignan; the French authorities say it's a nothing grape and are trying to marginalize it. Rubbish! It's an excellent, ancient, traditional grape when it's grown by the right people in the right place. This example, from right down towards Spain, has a wonderful deep red flavour, part fruit sauce, part savoury, part mountain herbs. Its acidity is fresh, its tannin is low, and there's just a little something of the sun-bleached rocky places where the old Carignan vines struggle to survive.

2008 Chilean Carmenère, Co-op/Fairtrade, Curicó Valley, Chile, 13.5% abv
Co-op, £4.99

There are some moves afoot in Chile to tame and civilize their wonderful, emotional Carmenère grape. But year after year this Co-op bottling delivers dollops of black fruit, chocolate syrup, leafy acidity and rippling peppercorn spice. Assertive, rich, with a bitter streak – don't change a thing. And remember – every Fairtrade wine you buy from the Co-op brings a double Fairtrade premium for the growers and producers, courtesy of the good old Co-op.

NV Rioja, Reciente (Bodegas Olarra), Spain, 13% abv
Sainsbury's, £4.99

Here come the good old days again – really tasty Rioja for a fiver. Sainsbury's have always had really nice own-label Rioja. They've changed their supplier, but if anything the quality has gone up – soft strawberry, the burst of leather, the rough kiss of peach skin, peppercorn and a hint of crème fraîche. If you want to show anyone why Rioja has remained such a favourite with us Brits for so long, serve them a bottle of this.

2007 Rioja, Vega Ariana, Spain, 13.5% abv
Waitrose, £4.99

It's wonderful to see affordable attractive Rioja back on our streets. Recently some cheap Rioja has just tasted cheap. This is much more like it. It's quite chunky, but is a buxom yet gentle mix of sultanas and toffee fudge with just a little strawberry and a dab of cream. Not subtle, but proper Rioja style.

CHEAP AND CHEERFUL

I wasn't sure I'd be able to include both these words in the same sentence. The past 12 months have seen an onslaught on budget wine drinkers. Many household incomes have been severely reduced at the same time as the government has taken great delight in portraying us as undeserving sinners against society and in taxing us ever more heavily for the misdemeanour of trying to enjoy a quiet drink to ease our troubles for an hour or two. The supermarkets meanwhile have been playing the role of villain and hero in about equal doses. They are using economic conditions in the UK to screw many of their producers ever closer to the ground, and producers who have a choice in the matter are saying they simply can't afford to do business with us any more. But the supermarket buyers have also managed to locate/create/magic a very decent array of wines at the bottom – or *near* the bottom end of the market. The absolute bottom of the barrel is as full of dregs as it has ever been. But between 3 and 4 pounds or so, what I hope is intelligent buying, rather than bullying, has produced a good crop of wines.

• In this section you will find white wines first, then reds, in descending price order.

WHITE WINE

2008 Chardonnay Reserve, Bushland, Hope Estate, Hunter Valley, New South Wales, Australia, 12.5% abv Aldi, £4.49

I don't know how they do it, but year after year Aldi and Hope Estate come up with classic Hunter Valley flavours for half the price they ought to be. Hunter is a really serious wine area north of Sydney; its wines have a very particular character. So do try this – a mellow, waxy white with a fascinating savoury taste like the core of a guava, gentle fruit like the flesh of a Golden Delicious or a white peach just a day short of ripeness, and a sappiness like the flesh just under the skin of a green melon.

• Aldi also has a big, rich, Hunter Valley Shiraz for the same price.

2008 Pinot Grigio-Chardonnay, Monte Cappella, Nagyréde, Hungary, 12.5% abv Morrisons, £4.45

Hungary is one of Europe's most ancient wine nations, and one of its least appreciated. One reason we don't drink Hungarian wines is that, if the label is in the native tongue, well, we've got no chance. But this label is simple, and the wine is delightful, its soft apple fruit smartened up with zesty lemon acidity and a smack of new leather to give it some style.

NV Vin de Pays des Côtes de Gascogne, South-West France, 11.5% abv Sainsbury's, £3.79

The best area for French bargain whites, snappy and fresh, is Gascony in South-West France. You'll find good examples under several titles, all vins de pays: Côtes de Gascogne, Gers and Comté Tolosan are the most likely ones. They're reliable, they're bright and fruity. The only caveat is that occasionally the producers sweeten the odd one up a bit for us Brits. I wish they wouldn't. They're far better dry. At the moment the Sainsbury's one is particularly sharp, zinging with grapefruit and green apple and lemon zest.

RED WINE

2008 Cuvée de Richard, Vin de Pays de l'Aude, Languedoc, France, 12% abv Majestic, £4.39

Penny-pinchers' paradise: full purply-red, low in tannin, rich in texture, pumping with juicy raspberry and blueberry fruit and possessing that precious jewel in a red wine – the ability to refresh, to stimulate, to recover your spirits and look life straight in the eye. And it's only 12% alcohol. Perhaps that's the secret.

2008 Merlot, Soleado, Valle Central, Chile, 12.5% abv Marks & Spencer, £4.29

Good stuff from M&S. They've persuaded one of Chile's top winemakers – Adolfo Hurtado of the dynamic Cono Sur winery – to craft this tasty little mouthful for them, and he's come up with a fresh, gentle, breezy red packed with plums and strawberries, and just as juicy as a Merlot ought to be but so rarely is.

2008 Malbec (Trivento), Mendoza, Argentina, 13% abv Asda, £4.24

Argentine Malbecs are by nature ripe, chubby-cheeked reds, and there are some pretty good ones on the shelves at around £4. But this is a notch up. It's made by Trivento, the Argentine branch of Chilean giant Concha y Trio, and uses grapes from some quite serious vineyards in the cooler parts of Mendoza, in the foothills of the Andes. The quality shines through. This has a dark, syrupy, plum fruit, clove spice, and enough of a bitter bite to have you crying out for a slab of beef to barbecue.

2008 Classic Côtes du Rhône, Rhône Valley, France, 12.5% abv Waitrose, £3.99

This isn't the most powerful or complex Côtes du Rhone you'll come across, but if you like the 'classic' flavours of juicy strawberry, hillside herbs and sunny, rocky minerals, you've just found this year's red.

2008 Corbières, Réserve de la Perrière, Mont Tauch, Languedoc, France, 13% abv
Waitrose, £3.99

Spanking good red packed with the juice of cranberries and strawberries, scuffed with mountain stones and scented with hillside herbs. Corbières is one of *la France profonde*'s last vinous outposts, full of ancient grapevines, and with just enough modern winemakers to make the best of them.

2008 Spanish Garnacha-Shiraz, Cariñena, Spain, 12% abv Marks & Spencer, £3.99

Cariñena has traditionally produced rather chunky, stolid reds, but the vines are old and excellent – all it needed was some decent winemaking. And here it is: bright, soft, but dry strawberryish fruit, a touch more tannin than you get in some modern Spanish reds, and a swish of herbs from the local tapas bar.

2007 Gran López Tinto (Crianzas y Viñedos Santo Cristo), Campo de Borja, Aragón, Spain, 14% abv Waitrose, £3.99

These Campo de Borja wines are an absolute joy: ripe, rumbustious, juicy, pleasure-filled reds with real character but no intellectual demands, Rich, chunky loganberry jam and raspberry sauce plus fistfuls of stones and a splattering of hillside herbs. You want recession red? Here it is.
• They do a pretty good Gran López white, too.

2008 Italian Vino da Tavola Rosso, Italy, 13% abv Marks & Spencer, £3.99

Vina da tavola simply means table wine, and it can hide a multitude of drecky flavours. But not when the wine is made by Gaetane Carron, a Frenchwoman I first met in Chile, and she clearly hasn't forgotten her New World lessons. The red blends four grape varieties, and you can really taste the deep, serious plum and cherry richness of Nero d'Avola and Syrah.
• The white is 60% Catarratto from Sicily and is a soft, full, dry, appley style with a clever whiff of nutmeg.

NV Sainsbury's Australian Shiraz, South Eastern Australia, 13.5% abv Sainsbury's, £3.99

Sainsbury's deserves a slap on the back for its own-label Aussie reds. This is really nice Shiraz
– plummy, spicy, scented, with the vanilla icing softness of angel cake.
• The Australian Merlot (£3.69) is plummy, blackcurranty and scented with eucalyptus.

2008 Trinacria Rosso, IGT Sicilia, Italy, 12% abv Waitrose, £3.99

This red is so bright and juicy and scented with rosehip syrup it makes me marvel at how Sicily
– a warm region – is becoming expert at cool, fresh wines, both cheap and expensive.
• The white Trinacria is an attractive, full, waxy white with a suggestion of apple blossom.

2008 Gran Tesoro Garnacha (Bodegas Borsao), Campo de Borja, Aragón, Spain, 13.5% abv
Booths, £3.89, Tesco, £3.54

Campo de Borja is a name you simply must look out for on labels of Spanish red.
It's never expensive, it's always good, and if any other hot countries with too many
grapes and not enough consumers would copy Campo de Borja, the world would never be short of good
red grog. Rich, dense fruit, yet marvellously juicy. Ripe strawberry, with the pips, plus some herbs and
a meaty spice. You heard it here first. Buy it.
• Gran Tesoro white and rosé are also good.

2008 Sainsbury's Chilean Merlot, 13.5% abv Sainsbury's, £3.29

Chile is the most reliable New World producer of good-quality budget reds. Merlot and Cabernet Sauvignon
are the grapes to look for. Tesco's and Asda's cheapies are pretty good, but my favourite is from Sainsbury's.
It's juicy and slightly syrupy, yet properly dry, with a punchy black plum flavour and a whiff of savoury scent.

ROSÉ WINES

It's one of the most appetizing sights in wine. You walk into
a bright, airy tasting room, and there, against a white wall
bathed in daylight flowing through a north-facing window,
is a line of pinks, from palest onion-skin through salmon
and sweetpea, strawberry, cherry and lurid day-glo clubber's
pink – your mouth waters with anticipation. We Brits are really
into pink at the moment: it's just about the fastest-growing
category of wine nationwide. OK, a lot of it is sweet Californian
sugar water – but a lot of it isn't. Pink's never been better.
Here's my pink pick.

• The wines are listed in descending price order.

2008 Corse Sartène Rosé, Domaine Saparale, Corsica, France, 13% abv Yapp Brothers, £11.75

Wow! This is wild. And so it should be. Corsica's a wild place. So wild that on my first visit the savagery of the wine – that's not necessarily a compliment – had me sticking to Campari and soda after the first day. But this is sort of bourgeois wild, suburban wild – wild custard, wild strawberry jam tart, wild shortbread, wild apple pie. See what I mean? No? It all made sense when I first wrote my notes: apple peel, strawberry, anis from the mountains and – I'm off again – wild Victoria sponge cake mixture. Try it.

2008 English Rosé (Chapel Down), Kent, 11.5% abv Marks & Spencer, £9.99

I don't care that summer 2008 was miserable. Well, I do – I spent it travelling round the UK in a tiny leaking caravan with a hairy petrolhead of dubious personal habits. I know how damp it was. But this rosé is a shining example of how English winemakers can now deal with rubbish weather and still make lovely stuff. This couldn't be more English – the scented crispness of an English Cox's apple, the mellow indulgence of strawberries and cream, and the lingering hedgerow perfume of elderflower.

2008 Tavel, Jean Oliver, Château d'Aquéria, Rhône Valley, France, 13.5% abv Waitrose, £9.79

Frankly, I've always thought that Tavel is not much more than a migraine lurking in wait. Thick, alcoholic, orangey-red, just over the road from Châteauneuf-du-Pape; why didn't they just make a red? But things are changing. This is still alcoholic – the predominant Grenache grape sees to that – but there are six other grapes, three red, three white, contributing to the mix, and this Tavel has stumbled into the 21st century, managing to be powerful, spicy, overbearing, yet marvellously fresh. Maybe the migraine won't hurt so much.

2008 Cabernet Sauvignon Rosé, Mulderbosch, Stellenbosch, South Africa, 13.5% abv
Armit, £9.25

Whatever red grape it's made from, there's a sort of blind-tasting test that rarely fails: if it smells smoky, it's probably from the Cape. This smells smoky. Hey, that's not a bad thing – think of barbecues and bonfires and log fires in winter – it's just a fact of life. And you'll like the wine – the gentle strawberry fruit and mellow, vaguely baked cream softness goes rather well with a whiff of smoke.

2007 Merlot-Malbec Rosé, Esk Valley, Hawkes Bay, New Zealand, 14% abv
Flagship Wines, nzhouseofwine.co.uk, WoodWinters, £8.99

Unlike Provence rosés, New World pinks can have a bit too much flavour, and looking at this ruddy, reddy-pink wine, you know it's no shrinking petal. In fact it's almost viscous, but the flavour is lovely – ripe apple juice, rich strawberries and cream, syrupy, glyceriny, indulgent. But the wine needs to be cold. Or the day needs to be cold. One or other.

2008 Côtes de Provence, Château Saint Baillon, Provence, France, 13% abv Goedhuis, £8.53

Provence rosés are famously pale. That used to be infamously pale, because their virtual lack of colour was matched by an almost complete lack of flavour. And their price was ridiculous. No one with any sense drank them. But they've undergone a sea change. They're still ludicrously expensive, they're still myopically pale – but their texture and flavour are delightful. This one is scented with apple blossom, and its pale fruit is as refreshing as the juice of a crisp apple running down your chin. But above all it's the lush, chubby texture that does the trick.

2008 Syrah, Vin de Pays des Côtes de Thongue, Domaine Saint Pierre, Languedoc, France, 12.5% abv Laithwaites, £6.79

The Syrah grape gives a lot of flavour to a rosé and you can sometimes wish it wasn't quite so assertive. But it works here. The colour is a fresh, vivid pink and there's a smell of apple orchards in bloom. It tastes good too, creamy strawberries mingling with apple peel acidity and juicy apple fruit – and there's a tiny prickle on your tongue that is rather refreshing.

2008 Viña Sol Rosé, Torres, Catalunya, Spain, 13.5% abv Tesco, Waitrose, £5.99, Wine Rack, £7.99 (3 for 2 £5.33)

I've been a fan of the white Viña Sol for years. Sometimes, in the depths of deepest Spain, an ice-cold Viña Sol has been the only thing that stood between me and thirst-crazed delirium. The pink is a more recent venture, but it works, with good, gentle, ripe strawberry fruit, a little pear flesh and a rather minerally acidity. Certainly good enough to relieve my thirst in an English summer.

2008 Bordeaux Rosé, Domaine de Sours, Bordeaux, France, 13% abv
Sainsbury's, £5.99

Bordeaux is famous for red wine, but at this price level it makes far better whites and pinks. Merlot and Cabernet Sauvignon are the main red wine grapes, but if you pick them a bit early, crush them and let the juice and skins mingle for just a day or so, and then make the wine as though it were a white, you get this come-hither pale pink colour, a scent of blackcurrant leaves, crisp apple fruit and a stony, refreshing dryness grazed with the acidity of apple peel.

NV La Brouette Rosé, Vin de Pays du Comté Tolosan, Producteurs Plaimont, South-West France, 12.5% abv
Corney & Barrow, £5.99

Very bright, bouncy wine. Loads of slightly squashy, slightly bruised fruit (beware over-enthusiastic bouncing), but that squashy flavour is actually rather nice – squashed bananas? pears going a bit gooey? Well, this is pears and apples and a touch of peach – not really pink flavours, but it works.

2008 Tarragona, Terramar Rosado, De Muller, Catalunya, Spain, 13% abv
Morrisons, £4.44

They'll make rosé out of whatever red grape they can find in Spain. This tasty little number
comes from Tempranillo and Cabernet Sauvignon, rather better known for mighty reds,
and it was made in Tarragona, originally famous for communion wine. This is a bit
lighthearted for 8 o'clock on a Sunday morning, but come brunchtime its soft, fresh
strawberry and apple gluggability could well affect your next week's state of grace.

2008 Las Falleras Rosé, Utiel-Requena, Valencia, Spain, 11.5% abv
Marks & Spencer, £3.99

Utiel-Requena is a baking area inland from Valencia – but clock that alcohol level:
11.5%. That means the grapes were picked early, before they'd baked all their
brightness away. It works. This has lots of decent strawberry and apple fruit,
fair acidity and even a slight bitter nip from the grape skins. And it's fresh.

2007 Viña Decana, Utiel-Requena Rosado, Valencia, Spain, 12% abv
Aldi, £3.99

If you've ever been to this part of Spain you'll know how hot it can get. It takes
a lot of skill to make attractive reds in that heat, let alone bright, breezy pinks.
But these guys have managed it. This wine isn't light and delicate – it's got
quite a rich, squashy apple flavour with a hint of peach – and it's not totally
dry. But there's good gritty peach-skin acidity and, though you can feel the
heat on the fruit, it's still fresh.

Keeping it light

We're becoming increasingly disenchanted with high-alcohol wines. So, increasingly, I'm checking the alcohol content of the wines I recommend. Here are my suggestions for drinks with fab flavours that won't leave you fuzzy-headed the next morning.

More and more wines seem to be hitting our shores at 14%, 15% – a couple of wines in this year's tastings came in at 16%. Red table wines! How can you enjoy that as a jolly beverage to knock back with your lamb chops: you'll be asleep or drunk before you've got the meat off the barbie.

Now, some wines have traditionally been high alcohol, and wear their strength well, but there are far too many wines that – less than a decade ago – used to perform at 11.5–12.5% alcohol and which are now adding at least a degree – and often more – to their strength, seemingly in an effort to ape the ripe round flavours of the New World. Thank goodness there are still a significant number showing more restraint.

At 12.5% there are lots of wines, particularly from cooler parts of France – most Beaujolais is 12–12.5% – northern Italy, where the most famous examples would be the Veneto reds Valpolicella and Bardolino and the white Soave, and from numerous parts of Eastern Europe, particularly Hungary.

But we've set the bar at 12%. This cuts out a lot of red wines; the slightly tart, refreshing white styles that sit easily at 12% can develop better flavour at a lower strength than most reds can. This exercise reminded us that Germany is full of fantastic Riesling wines as low as 7.5%. Muscadet is usually only 12%. Most supermarket house reds and whites are 11.5–12%. Western Australian whites are often 12%. And Champagne, along with most other sparkling wines, is only 12%. Hallelujah.

• VdP = Vin de Pays

White wine

- 2008 Airén-Sauvignon Blanc, Gran López, La Mancha, Spain, £3.99, Waitrose, 11% abv
- 2008 Aligoté, Blason de Bourgogne, Burgundy, France, £8.99, Waitrose, 12% abv
- 2008 Bacchus, Chapel Down, Kent, England, c.£10, widely available, 12% abv
- 2008 Bordeaux Sauvignon Blanc, Calvet Limited Release, France, £5.49, Waitrose, 11.5% abv
- 2007 Bordeaux Sauvignon-Sémillon, Château La Freynelle, France, £8.49, Oxford Wine Co, 12% abv
- 2007 Chablis, Burgundy, France, £9.99, Marks & Spencer, 12% abv
- 2007 Chablis, Domaine la Vigne Blanche, Burgundy, France, £8.99, Aldi, 12% abv (page 54)
- 2007 Chardonnay Bourgogne, Jurassique, Jean-Marc Brocard, Burgundy, France, £7.99, Booths, 12% abv (page 57)
- 2008 Chardonnay (Tyrrell's), Hunter Valley, New South Wales, Australia, £7.99, Marks & Spencer, 11.5% abv
- 2008 Chardonnay-Semillon, The Harbour, New South Wales, Australia, £9.99, Tesco, 12% abv
- 2008 Chenin Blanc, La Grille, Loire Valley, France, £5.99, Majestic, 11% abv (page 86)
- 2008 Chenin-Colombard, Domaine Maurel, VdP d'Oc, Languedoc-Roussillon, France, £8.99 (3 for 2 £5.99), Wine Rack, 12% abv
- 2008 Colombard-Sauvignon Blanc, La Biondina, Primo Estate, McLaren Vale, South Australia, £8.99, AustralianWineCentre.co.uk, 12% abv (page 54)
- 2008 VdP des Côtes de Gascogne, Colombelle, Producteurs Plaimont, South-West France, £6.20, Caves de Pyrene, 11.5% abv
- 2008 VdP des Côtes de Gascogne, Domaine de Plantérieu, South-West France, £4.99, Waitrose, 11% abv
- VdP des Côtes de Gascogne, South-West France, £3.79, Sainsbury's, 11.5% abv (page 98)
- 2008 Cuvée Pêcheur, VdP du Comté Tolosan, South-West France, £3.99, Waitrose, 11.5% abv
- 2007 Cuvée de Richard, VdP du Comté Tolosan, South-West France, £3.79, Majestic, 11.5% abv
- 2008 Gavi, Quatro Sei, Piedmont, Italy, £6.49, Marks & Spencer, 11.5% abv
- 2008 VdP du Gers, Lesc, Producteurs Plaimont, South-West France, £5.40, Caves de Pyrene, 11.5% abv (page 88)
- 2008 VdP du Gers, Pujalet, South-West France, £4.99, Waitrose, 11.5% abv
- 2008 Malvasia, Carletti, Abruzzo, Italy, £5.99, Oddbins, 12% abv
- 2008 (Spanish) Macabeo, Cariñena, Spain, £3.99, Marks & Spencer, 12% abv
- 2007 Moulin de Gassac, VdP de l'Hérault, Mas de Daumas Gassac, Languedoc-Roussillon, France, £6.92, Averys, 12% abv
- 2008 Muscadet Côtes de Grandlieu sur lie, Fief Guérin, Loire Valley, France, £5.99, Waitrose, 12% abv
- 2007 Muscadet Sèvre et Maine sur lie, André-Michel Brégeon, Loire Valley, France, £7.57, Goedhuis, 12% abv (page 63)
- 2005 Muscadet Sèvre et Maine sur lie, Cuvée des Ceps Centenaires, Ch. de Chasseloir, Loire Valley, France, £7.95, FromVineyardsDirect.com, 12% abv (page 62)
- 2008 Muscadet Sèvre et Maine sur lie, Taste the Difference (Jean Douillard), Loire Valley, France, £5.99, Sainsbury's, 11.5% abv

- 2008 L'Orangerie, Vin de Savoie, Philippe & François Tiollier, France, £8.50, Yapp Brothers, 11% abv (page 56)
- 2008 Orvieto, Cardeto, Umbria, Italy, £4.99, Waitrose, 12% abv
- 2007 Petit Chablis, Cave des Vignerons, Burgundy, France, £9.99, Waitrose, 11.5% abv
- 2007 Pinot Bianco delle Venezie, Canto Bianco, Endrezzi, Trentino, Italy, £6.99, Adnams, 12% abv
- 2007 Pinot Blanc-Auxerrois, Albert Mann, Alsace, France, £11, Caves de Pyrene, 12% abv (page 46)
- 2007 Pinot Grigio, Budavar, Hungary, £3.49, Aldi, 11.5% abv
- 2008 Riesling, Tim Adams, Clare Valley, South Australia, £8.99, AustralianWineCentre.co.uk, Tesco, 11.5% abv
- 2008 Riesling, Autumn Picked, Marlborough, New Zealand, £7.99, Tesco, 8.5% abv
- 2006 Riesling, The Doctor's, Forrest Estate, Marlborough, New Zealand, £8.99, Adnams, 9.5% abv
- 2006 Riesling Kabinett, Ayler Kupp, Margaretenhof Weingut Weber, Mosel, Germany, £7.99, Majestic, 9.5% abv (page 50)
- 2004 Riesling Kabinett, Scharzhofberger, Reichsgraf von Kesselstatt, Mosel, Germany, £8.99, Co-op, 8.5% abv (page 54)
- 2008 Riesling, Dr L, Loosen, Mosel, Germany, £6–7, widely available, 8.5% abv
- 2007 Riesling, Mineralstein, Germany, £6.99, Marks & Spencer, 12% abv
- 2008 Riesling, Opou Vineyard, Millton, Gisborne, New Zealand, £11.50, Vintage Roots, 8.5% abv (page 46)
- 2008 Riesling, Private Bin, Villa Maria, Marlborough, New Zealand, £7.99, Booths, Majestic, nzhouseofwine.co.uk, 12% abv (page 60)
- 2006 Riesling, Rippon, Central Otago, New Zealand, £14.95, Lea and Sandeman, 11.3% abv
- 2007 Riesling, Steillage, Mosel, Germany, £5.99, Tesco Finest, 11.5% abv
- 2008 Riesling, Tingleup, Great Southern, Western Australia, £6.99, Tesco Finest, 12% abv
- 2008 Riesling, Waipara West, Waipara, New Zealand, £8.95, Waterloo Wine Co, 10% abv (page 55)
- 2008 Saumur, Les Andides, Loire Valley, France, £6.49, Waitrose, 12% abv
- 2007 Sauvignon Blanc, Champteloup, Touraine, Loire Valley, France, £6.49, Waitrose, 12% abv
- 2008 Sauvignon Blanc, Jacques Lurton Selection, VdP du Val de Loire, France, £4.99, Sainsbury's, 11.5% abv
- 2008 Sauvignon, VdP du Val de Loire, Lacheteau, France, £4.99, Marks & Spencer, 12% abv
- 2007 Sauvignon Blanc, St-Bris, William Fèvre, Burgundy, France, £8.99, Waitrose, 12% abv
- 2008 Sauvignon Blanc-Gros Manseng, Les Montgolfiers, VdP des Côtes de Gascogne, South-West France, £6.99, Tesco, 12% abv
- 2003 Semillon, Allandale, Hunter Valley, New South Wales, Australia, £11.99, Oz Wines, 12% abv (page 22)
- 2006 Semillon, Denman Vineyard, Hunter Valley, New South Wales, Australia, £7.09, Tesco Finest, 10.5% abv (page 64)
- 2005 Semillon, Fox Hollow, Hunter Valley, New South Wales, Australia, £18, Marks & Spencer, 11.5% abv (page 40)
- 2008 Semillon-Sauvignon Blanc, See Saw, South Australia, £7.99, Waitrose, 12% abv
- 2008 Semillon-Sauvignon Blanc, Vasse Felix, Margaret River, Western Australia, £9.99, Waitrose, 12% abv

- 2007 Soave Classico, Italy, £3.98, Asda, 12% abv
- 2008 Torrontes, Norton, Mendoza, Argentina, £5.99, Oddbins, 12% abv
- 2008 Trinacria Bianco, Sicily, Italy, £3.99, Waitrose, 12% abv
- 2008 Verdicchio dei Castelli di Jesi, Castellani, Italy, £4.05, Asda, 12% abv
- 2008 Vieille Fontaine, VdP d'Oc, Languedoc-Roussillon, France, £3.29, Tesco, 11.5% abv
- 2007 Villa Antinori, Tuscany, Italy, £7.99, Morrisons, 12% abv
- 2008 Viña Esmeralda, Torres, Catalunya, Spain, c.£7, widely available, 11.75% abv
- 2008 Viña Sol, Torres, Catalunya, Spain, c.£6.50, widely available, 11.5% abv
- 2008 Vinho Verde, Quinta de Azevedo, Portugal, £6, Majestic, Waitrose, 10.5% abv (page 86)
- 2008 The White Mullet, Pikes, Clare Valley, South Australia, £9.99, Wine Rack, 12% abv (page 71)

Rosé wine

- 2008 Côtes de Provence, Domaine de Buganay, Provence, France, £7.99, Waitrose, 12% abv
- 2008 Cuvée Fleur, VdP de l'Hérault, Languedoc-Roussillon, France, £3.79, Waitrose, 11.5% abv
- 2008 English Rosé (Chapel Down), £9.99, Marks & Spencer, 11.5% abv (page 103)
- 2008 Las Falleras, Utiel-Requena, Valencia, Spain, £3.99, Marks & Spencer, 11.5% abv (page 107)
- VdP du Gard, Baron St-Jean, Languedoc-Roussillon, France, £2.99, Aldi, 12% abv
- 2008 Utiel-Requena Rosado, Viña Decana, Valencia, Spain, £3.99, Aldi, 12% abv (page 107)

Red wine

- Beaujolais (Sainsbury's), France, £3.99, 12% abv
- 2007 Bordeaux Supérieur, Château David, Bordeaux, France, £5.49, Sainsbury's, 12% abv
- 2008 VdP des Côtes de Gascogne, South-West France, £4.99, Marks & Spencer, 12% abv
- 2008 Cuvée Chasseur, VdP de l'Hérault, Languedoc-Roussillon, France, £3.69, Waitrose, 12% abv
- 2008 Cuvée de Richard, VdP de l'Aude, Languedoc-Roussillon, France, £4.39, Majestic, 12% abv (page 99)
- 2008 Gamay, VdP de l'Ardèche (Cave St-Désirat), Rhône Valley, France, £3.99, Marks & Spencer, 12% abv
- 2008 Gamay Noir, Woodthorpe Vineyard, Te Mata Estate, Hawkes Bay, New Zealand, c.£10.95, Waitrose, others, 12% abv (page 100)
- 2008 (Spanish) Garnacha-Shiraz, Cariñena, Spain, £3.99, Marks & Spencer, 12% abv
- Gran Valero, Cariñena, Co-op San Bernabe, Spain, £5.49, Wine Rack, 12% abv
- 2006 Marcillac, Cuvée Laïris, Jean-Luc Matha, South-West France, £9.50, Caves de Pyrene, 12% abv (page 73)
- 2007 St-Nicolas-de-Bourgueil, Les Graviers, Frédéric Mabileau, Loire Valley, France, £10.99, Corney & Barrow, 12% abv (page 66)
- 2006 Syrah, VdP de l'Ardèche, Cave St-Désirat, Rhône Valley, France, £4.99, Booths, 12% abv
- 2008 Trinacria Rosso, Sicily, Italy, £3.99, Waitrose, 12% abv (page 101)
- 2008 Valpolicella (Asda), Italy, £3.38, Asda, 12% abv
- 2007 Valpolicella, Adalia, Veneto, Italy, £10.99, Oddbins, 12% abv
- Valpolicella (Sainsbury's), Italy, £3.42, Sainsbury's, 11.5% abv

FIZZ

We should need fizz more than ever in these dark days. And one of the old adages of the wine world is that Champagne sales hold up or even increase during recession times. Well, not this year: Champagne sales have dropped 15% in the past year – and the UK is Champagne's biggest export market. The reason is, I'm sure, partly because this recession, unlike other recent ones, has been so bitter and socially divisive that people are shunning ostentation, and no number of glasses of fizz at home with your beloved is going to make up for the undrunk pyramids of Champagne piled up in bars and restaurants up and down the country waiting for the traders and bankers and good-time Charlies to return. But have you noticed the prices, especially of the big brands? Some of them are £5 a bottle dearer than this time last year. That's the Champagne business all over. Kick your most loyal customer when he's down – and we are their most loyal customer. So it's funny that the wine trade is full of whispers about large stocks of unsold fizz in Champagne itself, and discounts of 25% and more if any trader will buy. Who's taking the piss out of us consumers? When it comes to Champagne, it sometimes feels as though everybody is. Well, I've still included my favourite Champagnes here, but they're outnumbered 2 to 1 by other sparklers that offer just as much fun for a more affordable price.

• The wines are listed in descending price order.

2002 Champagne, Blanc de Blancs Grand Cru, Le Mesnil, France, 12% abv
Berry Bros, £30.99, Waitrose, £29.99

What a combination. The magnificent vintage of 2002 and the even more magnificent vineyards of Le Mesnil, where Chardonnay grows more scented, more elegant, more perfectly balanced between cream and hazelnut and lemon than anywhere else in Champagne. Only 1996 beats 2002 as a vintage since 1990, but one of the drawbacks of such quality is that the Champagne needs to age. This beautiful wine is still lusty and ebullient, and really needs 3–4 years to lose its bluster and bravado and settle in to a long, calm maturity. You could easily age this for 10 years, and the yeasty cream, the brioche, the hazelnut and oatmeal dabbed with chocolate will gradually all come together in a paean of praise to the greatness of Chardonnay fruit from the precious slopes of Le Mesnil.

NV Champagne, Brut Zero, Tarlant, France, 12% abv
Marks & Spencer, £28

You have to be confident to make a Champagne like this – Brut Zero means there's no sugar added to soften the wine, to smooth out the harsh edge of acidity most Champagne naturally has. This is Champagne

as naked as nature intended. Sugar is the new clothes the Emperor didn't get. It's a shock, but it's a good one. So are you ready? Can you cope? The apples are lean, the nuts are lean, the cream is lean, even the bubbles are lean and the spice is shiveringly dry. These are the true flavours of Champagne, minus the make-up.

NV Champagne, Grand Cru Blanc de Blancs Brut, R & L Legras, France, 12% abv Lea and Sandeman, £24.95

Good, assertive, rather grand Champagne. It comes from very swish vineyards near Epernay, and certainly isn't any old party pop, but for a celebration of something serious – like your 100th wedding anniversary or the reversal of the magnetic North Pole – this would be the perfect stuff. It has a very traditional flavour of baked apples, slightly bruised, sitting in the roasting tin, basking in their own syrup and waiting for a dollop of crème fraîche. The acidity is insistent but not aggressive; this is very attractive, haughty, well-bred fizz – if 'fizz' is the right word for such an adult wine.

NV Champagne, Premier Cru Brut, Pierre Vaudon (Union Champagne), France, 12% abv Haynes Hanson & Clark, £23.85

I've enjoyed more parties with this than with any other Champagne. Whenever I see the Vaudon label, I immediately relax in the knowledge that the host cares about his guests – and that if everything else goes wrong, well, I'm all right, so long as the wine doesn't give out. Gentle, mellow, fluffy apple blending with crème fraîche, hazelnut and brioche crust. Beautifully balanced, leaving you with a contented understanding of why you paid Champagne prices.

NV Quartet Brut, Roederer Estate, Anderson Valley, California, USA, 12% abv Majestic, Quaff, Waitrose and others, £19.99

Roederer could lay claim to being the finest of the well-known Champagne houses, and when they set up an operation in an obscure, isolated northern Californian valley, surrounded by forest, wild woodsmen and a never-ending blanket of fog shuttling backwards and forwards across their vineyards, it was

because the dismal conditions reminded them of Champagne. Their objective was to do their damnedest to make Champagne in America's Golden West – or rather, in this case, its misty, miserable, windswept, Champagne-like west. They've done a superb job. The wine is a little fuller than a typical Champagne, but it has the classic fruit quality of loft apples or baked apples. It even has a little blossoming scent and the unmistakable nutty, yeasty, gentle, smooth texture of the finest Champagne.

NV Champagne, Brut Selection, Marc Chauvet, France, 12% abv
The Real Wine Company, £19.99

This has a full, rollicking, jolly quality to it, hedonism to the fore, a big smile on your face, optimism in your eyes, and all the typical Champagne flavours a bit exaggerated. The loft apples are blowsy and turning to tasty mush as they bake, the brioche has transformed into a syrupy French baba sponge, and the acidity has sidled across to something more shiny and metallic than harsh and lean.

NV Vintage Reserve Brut, Chapel Down, Kent, UK, 12% abv
Waitrose, £16.99, Wine Rack, £19.99 (3 for 2 £13.33)

Oh, to be in England when the hedgerows smell like this – and the bright optimism of spring is reflected in the foaming rush of bubbles and the utter, joyous Englishness of the wine. This fizz could only be English and makes no attempt to ape another style – Champagne, for instance. English sparkling wine has built a formidable reputation over the past few years for excellent fizz that's indistinguishable from, or even better than, French Champagne. But there's another style of fizz in Blighty – one that tastes utterly English. This positively reeks of elderflower and the flavour keeps elderflower to the fore, packing hedgerow sap and hawthorn blossom, greengages and a mild bitterness halfway between tree bark and almond skins into a single mouthful. Unmistakably English in every way, except that it's making my stiff upper lip quiver with delight.

• Marks & Spencer's English Sparkling Reserve Brut (£16.99), from the same winemaker, has the same elderflower freshness – and the bubbles are sheer class.

NV Champagne, Blanc de Noirs Brut, France, 12% abv
Sainsbury's, £15.99

Most Champagnes are made from a blend of black grapes and white. Black grapes provide a round, rather fat and solid texture to the wine, while white grapes provide zip and delicacy. Blend them together and it should be about right. Even so, some producers have always made a speciality of wine using only white or black grapes. Blanc de Blancs is a reasonably common style. Blanc de Noirs, from black grapes, is much rarer, because the effects can be just too plump and rather unrefreshing. But Sainsbury's has always managed to source a good example, and this year's offering is gentle, rather mellow, the apple fruit is a little riper than usual, the cream is quite thick and spicy and there's just a hint of chocolate as you swallow the wine.

NV Pelorus, Cloudy Bay, New Zealand, 12.5% abv Adnams, Berry Bros, Harvey Nichols, Majestic, Waitrose and others, c.£14

Cloudy Bay is part of the Louis Vuitton luxury luggage group, which also owns the Champagne house of Veuve Clicquot. So you could think of Pelorus as Veuve Clicquot from the Land of the Long White Cloud (ie New Zealand). This is outstanding fizz; I wish Veuve Clicquot was a) this price, and b) so consistently delicious, but it fails on both counts. So enjoy this Kiwi version instead – beautifully creamy, smelling of macaroons and hazelnuts, fresh and foaming, but with the soft reassurance of baked rice pudding.

NV Prosecco Valdobbiadene, Extra Dry, Villa Sandi, Veneto, Italy, 11% abv
Playford Ros, £11.52

Prosecco is a crowd pleaser. That's its only job. Not to be complex, not to be taken too seriously, and frankly, not to be commented on – except to say, this is the real thing! Foaming bubbles, lovely not-quite-dry Cox's apple and Williams' pear flesh fruit, mellow acidity like boiled lemons, and a puff of freshen-up scent like a sappy lily stem.

NV Prosecco, Casa Sant'Orsola, Italy, 11.5% abv
Wine Rack, £10.99 (3 for 2 £7.33)

Bright, breezy, fresh and foaming – just what I want Prosecco to be. Although it's more expensive than Cava, Prosecco sales are rocketing, because, frankly, Cava can be pretty hard work, while Prosecco is party pop in spades. This has delightful pear fruit, mild acidity and a slight scent of fresh clean leather. And it foams all round your mouth and up to your brain.

2008 Sparkling Pinot Noir, Bird in Hand, Adelaide Hills, South Australia, 13% abv Tanners, £10.95

There's no culture cringe about this baby, certainly nothing Champagne-style, but it's good, precisely because it's so Australian. It's pale pink, and as soon as you smell it, you're in Aussie territory, eucalyptus scenting the white peach, strawberry and blackcurrant fruits. Blackcurrant? That's not a Pinot Noir taste, I agree. I'd have said they'd added some Shiraz or Cabernet – but I like it. You'll get a taste of mint, too, when you swallow it, along with the ripe fruit and some blackcurrant leaf acidity. Hmm. Cabernet again. Do I care? Hell, no.

NV Crémant de Loire, Brut, Jean-Marie Penet, Château de la Presle, Loire Valley, France, 12% abv Christopher Piper Wines, £10.80

Not your usual party fizz, but really interesting wine that happens to have bubbles coming through it. It's got a mildly floral soap scent with a wisp of cedar, and this scent and wood bark mellow quality continues in the flavour of the wine, which is waxy, leathery rather than sharp. Golden Delicious appley fruit (ie very mild) and a dollop of fresh farm cream make this a satisfying, rather contemplative glass of bubbles.

NV Crémant de Bourgogne Brut Rosé, Blason de Bourgogne, Caves de Bailly, Burgundy, France, 12% abv Waitrose, £9.99

You want good Champagne? You want sexy, seductive, pink Champagne? I've got it here. Whoops. It can't be Champagne. It tastes like it, it looks like it, it has the same grape varieties – but it's only £9.99. These grapes come from just over the 'administrative' boundary from Champagne, so are only worth a fraction of the price, even though they're just as good. Taste the wine – lovely juicy apple and strawberry fruit with a little red plum-skin nip of acid chewiness to liven things up. Good, gentle, yeasty cream just lightly scraped with stones, apple peel sharpness trying and nobly failing to make its presence felt. All for £9.99.

NV Prosecco Raboso, Italy, 11.5% abv Marks & Spencer, £7.99

Pink Prosecco? Hey, why not? Pink's fun. Fizz is fun. I know Prosecco's a white grape, but the Italians are breezily easygoing with such little matters as the grape being the wrong colour. Just add something else. Local – like the Raboso used here. Or from 1000 miles away – like in the example below, which uses Sicily's Nerello Mascalese for colour. So long as it's fun. Well, this is fun – bright, fresh pink, and the flavour and perfume is the usual mouthwatering pear and banana combo.
• Nerello Mascalese-Prosecco Brut (Waitrose, £7.99) has an attractive flavour like pears baked in white wine with ginger. Hmm. Good dessert idea.

2007 Lambrusco Reggiano, Autentico, Medici Ermete & Figli, Emilia-Romagna, Italy, 11% abv Marks & Spencer, £7.99

99.9% of the Lambrusco we see in this country is vapid sugar-water. Welcome to the world of the 0.1%. This is dark purple, with exotic, sexy, pink-purple foam. And it's dry! It has challenging, raw raspberries, red plums and sloe fruit, a bit of tannin and acidity, a smell of scented tree bark and sappy stems, and an undertow of dusty old wardrobes. It isn't that fizzy, and the truly authentic Lambruscos are slightly more sweet-sour. But this is well worth a try with proper spag Bolognese – it's Bologna's local wine.

NV Cava, Vineyard X Brut, Spain, 11.5% abv
Wine Rack, £7.49 (3 for 2 £4.99)

If you want Cava as a party fizz, this is currently the best, the cleanest, the fruitiest, the least hangover-inducing on the market. It's got an apple blossom scent – any scent in Cava is pretty good – easygoing, gentle apple flesh fruit with a touch of peach, lemon zest and a slightly yeasty soft finish to massage your palate. And at the 3 for 2 price you could really party.

2008 Moscato d'Asti, Sourgal, Elio Perrone, Piedmont, Italy, 5% abv
The Wine Society, £6.50

Talk about wine without tears. I mean, this is hardly wine, it's only 5% alcohol, but that's the point with Moscato d'Asti – they only half-ferment the gorgeous Muscat juice, and then bottle it, full of froth and the heady scent and sweetness of the grape. This smells like muscatel juice crushed straight from the fresh-plucked bunch. It has a fragrance halfway between unsmoked Virginia tobacco and spring flowers, its sweetness is like a nectar made of muscatel grapes and the flesh of a perfect white peach, and the whole dazzle-eyed pleasure bomb seems to be held together by a zesty acidity as scented and fresh as the finest Sorrento lemon. P.S. You'll need a corkscrew to remove the cork.

2006 Crémant du Jura, Chardonnay Brut, Philippe Michel, France, 12.5% abv Aldi, £5.99

Delightful and impressive fizz from the wild Jura mountains. They grow good Chardonnay there in their cool, misty mountain eyrie, and Chardonnay is what makes Blanc de Blancs Champagne. But the Jura guys charge £5.99, not £25.99 or more. And what they offer is a firm, fresh, savoury sparkler, foaming bubbles bursting through yeasty cream, apple fruit and a splash of honey. Tell your friends it's Champagne, if you must. The grape's the same, the bubbles are the same, the effect is the same. The price isn't.

NV Pinot Grigio Brut, Monte Cappella, Balatonboglari, Hungary, 11.5% abv Morrisons, £5.99

Hungary is so bursting with opportunity and so desperate to do business with us that I don't really mind that Morrisons have decided to label this as though it's from Italy – Monte Cappella Pinot Grigio – I'm just glad that they're giving us really nice fizz for a very affordable price. I'd like it a touch drier, but the fizz is good, and Hungarian Pinot Grigio is some of the tastiest in Europe; this has very attractive apple and honey fruit with an aftertaste like brioche, or fresh baked bread crust. If I had the slightest idea of what it was in Hungarian, I'd say 'cheers'.

2005 Cava, Mas Miralda Brut, Asda Extra Special, Spain, 11.5% abv Asda, £5

This is made by Codorníu (Spain's best big Cava company) – but so were several of the other supermarket Cavas we tasted, which were simply too raw and rough to enjoy. Maybe Asda takes Cava more seriously. In any case, this is pretty good – quite mature, with a hint of raisin ripeness, some good lemon and apple peel acidity and a stony, dry finish.

SWEETIES

I wonder whether we truly appreciate hard work and commitment way beyond the call of duty in this country. If we did, we might all take a bit more interest in sweet wines – genuinely sweet wines, not sugar-water pop like Liebfraumilch. These are exceedingly difficult to make: you have to take risks in leaving your grapes on the vine long after normal picking has finished. Which means you can lose your entire crop if the weather turns. And even the most obsessive of sweet wine makers admits that they make a dreadful mess of your winery and machinery. And after all that, does anyone want them? Is anyone prepared to pay the necessary high price for these beauties? Well, in the high street and in the supermarkets, I see less and less evidence of sweet wines on the shelves, and I wonder if the style is being left to wither. Supermarket buyers would defend themselves by saying, if there's no market, why should we stock them? I'd counter that by saying, if you don't stock them, how can we create a market? Meanwhile, several independent wine merchants have told me that they can't get enough good sweet wine; despite the high prices, the wines sell and they're expanding their range. This looks like one more niche market the smaller merchants are going to be able to colonize during our current turbulent times.

• The wines are listed in descending price order.

2008 Riesling, Cordon Cut, Mount Horrocks, Clare Valley, South Australia, 11% abv

Butlers Wine Cellar, Liberty, Martinez, Philglas & Swiggot, others, £17.95/37.5cl

The Aussies are a resourceful bunch. If you live in the Clare Valley, where the conditions are great for dry wines but no good for sweeties – but you are determined to make a sweetie – you improvise. You ripen your Riesling grapes, and then you snip the branch just before the bunch of grapes so that it hangs down limp, the sap doesn't get through, and the grapes shrivel on the vine. And when they shrivel all the sugar – and the acid – is intensified. So long as the grapes are good you'll get stunning rich wine. Well, Mount Horrocks dry Riesling is in Australia's Premier League, and their class shines through in this rich concoction, too. It's a beautiful bright green-gold, and a soaring perfume of violet, beeswax, leather and juicy golden peach rises out of the glass. The flavour's fabulous: runny honey sweetness, peaches in luscious syrup, loads of crackling crisp apple and lime zest fresh acidity and – as though the wine was getting embarrassed about being too rich and sweet – an almost austere scent of sappy lily stems and leather lingering in the unctuous heat of the wine.

2007 Weissburgunder Eiswein, Darting Estate, Pfalz, Germany, 9% abv

Marks & Spencer, £14.99/37.5cl

Eiswein is a wonderful rarity from Germany. They leave the grapes on the vine until the frosts of winter – usually December – bring the temperature down to a horrific −10°C. Then they send out anyone who has been rude to them during the past year to pick the grapes, usually before dawn. The grapes come in with all the water in them frozen solid, but the sugar and acids haven't frozen; they've just intensified. It may take all day to press this sugar out of the grapes while keeping the shards of ice from melting.

It may take two days. This is the result – a thrilling deep syrup of honey and acid. The honey-acid partnership is so invasive, it positively hurts your teeth, but the wonderful flavours of guavas, peach and superripe grapes, all swathed in syrup, make it worthwhile.

2006 Monastrell, Castaño Dulce, Bodegas Castaño, Yecla, Spain, 16% abv
Liberty Wines, £14.49/50cl

I could almost put this in the port section – perhaps I should have done – because that's what it resembles. This is a big, dark beast from one of Spain's hottest vineyard regions, down near Alicante. It has the same dense, rich, purple-black fruit of fine port but seems almost sweeter because there's barely any counter-balancing tannin and none of that rasping spirit that sometimes brings you up with a start in a port. Instead you get sensuous, rich black plum and blackberry fruit syrup and a good sprinkling of clove and cinnamon spice.

2005 Botrytis Riesling, Tamar Ridge, Tasmania, Australia, 9% abv
Vin du Van, £13.25/37.5cl

Tasmania is Australia's coolest state and it can be pretty damp as well – but reasonably often they get a lovely long warm autumn to ripen the vines as they roll down towards the Tamar River. If that sounds a bit like the conditions on the Rhine in Germany, you're not wrong. And as in Germany, if you wait, chewing your lip and tying good luck knots in your toggle, you can make great sweet wine. It's the balance between acidity and honey that makes Riesling sweeties so irresistible. Here you get gooey, runny honey intertwined with lime – the acid and oily scent of lime zest and the bitter-sweet attack of West Indian lime marmalade. And running beneath all this, like a fragile careworn cloud, is a half-visible lining of minerals, stones and linseed oil.

2008 Botrytis Riesling-Traminer, Joseph, La Magia, Primo Estate, South Australia, 11% abv
AustralianWineCentre.co.uk, £11.99/37.5cl

Trust Primo Estate's Joe Grilli to change all the rules about sweet Riesling being scented with lime blossom and scythed through with gum-thrilling acidity. Well, he is Italian; they do things differently there. Like mixing the droopy-eyed, sultry Traminer grape with the sharp, natty Riesling. And this creates a brilliant but unexpected wodge of flavours: the wine's fat and rich and has something of the sweet sourness of sherry; the yeasty flavour of fermentation is still lurking guiltily in the body of the wine, giving an almost meaty complexity to the rich peach fruit and the lime zest and lemon juice acidity (yes, there is some); and the waxy, leathery texture that will begin to take over this wine if you give it a few years' age.

NV Muscat, Rutherglen, Cellar No.9, Seppeltsfield, Victoria, Australia, 16.5% abv
Flagship Wines, Halifax Wine Co, Nidderdale and others, £11.99

I keep expecting us all to fall in love with these wonderful liqueur Muscats from Australia's gold rush region of Rutherglen. They're the absolute essence of so many of the sweet things we adore, and they manage to be unbelievably rich without being at all cloying, simply because they're so delicious. What about heavenly dates and raisins and dried figs? What about a celestial syrup made up of muscovado sugar and the sweetest muscat grapes on the planet? What about fruit cake and treacle pudding and Harrogate toffee? Yet always bright, never thick and dull; brown and old, yet always streaked with mouthwatering, lively acidity that will have you clamouring for a refill.

2006 Jurançon, Château Jolys, Cuvée Jean, South-West France, 13% abv
Waitrose, £10.99

This is a rare delight, harvested from tiny pockets of vines nestled high in the Pyrenean foothills, angled towards the sun, protected from the worst of the mountain weather. In the autumn and early winter a warm wind wafts up from the south and methodically dries the grapes on the vine, so that by the time they are harvested in November the sugar has been intensified – but so has the acid. The resulting wine is sweet but not *very* sweet – fat and waxy, almost as though it were coated with lanolin, pineapple sweet and streaked with the pure, uncomplicated acidity of fresh lemon juice.

2005 Pacherenc du Vic Bilh, Maestria, Producteurs Plaimont, South-West France, 13.5% abv
Tanners Wines, £7.90/50cl

Pacherenc du Vic Bilh, as its unwieldy title suggests, is an obscure wine – made in the deepest south-west of *la France profonde*. It can be either dry or sweet, but it was effectively extinct not so long ago. But the energetic and powerful local co-op, Producteurs Plaimont – who produce a lot of the cheap and snappy Vin de Pays des Côtes de Gascogne whites we so enjoy in the UK – decided to give it a go, and the result is impressive. It's not mainstream stuff, in fact it's a bit unnerving, with its sweet, tired fruit of quince and medlars and its sense of a damp, cool, autumn evening hanging about like tendrils of mist. But it's fascinating, old-style wine; not massively sweet – to drink by itself or with fruit – even its pineapple richness is edged with bitterness and its marmalade and fudge finish is streaked with a Puritan squirt of lemon.

FORTIFIED WINES

They say the sherry segment of our wine world is in inexorable decline. The most frequent reason given is that the traditional sherry enthusiasts are all dying off and not being replaced in a 'yoof'-obsessed world gone starry-eyed for Chardonnay and Sauvignon and Pinot Grigio rather than for the more 'adult' pleasures of a glass of dry fino sherry. But Spanish cuisine is on a roll at the moment. Tapas bars are some of the trendiest places to meet and nibble and drink. Sherry – especially dry sherry – is often the perfect tapas wine. If you're still a sherry virgin, get yourself a plate of salted almonds, some manchego cheese and deep-fried squid, and give it a go.

Port is the easy side of fortified wines. It's sweet, it's potent, it's succulent, brimming with natural fruit sugar, ripeness borne of long hot autumn days, some spices from Portugal's old trade routes, some fiery spirit to rack up the effects on your brain and your heart and to give muscle and masculinity to the brew. Well, that's the traditional view. Some modern ports seem to be playing down the 'muscle and masculinity' with a gentler, more scented style. I think there's room for both styles, so long as the gorgeous superripe indulgence of the flavour still dilutes your common sense and persuades you that one more glass won't do any harm.

• In this section you will find sherries first, then ports, in descending price order.

SHERRY

Amontillado, Tio Diego, Valdespino, 15% abv
Moreno Wine, £17.99

This is lovely sherry, but not yet quite back to its old form of a few years ago, when it had the wonderful, lush but dry, classic amontillado flavour of buttered brazils. Surprisingly for sherry, you can still detect traces of the American wood in which they fermented the base wine before it spent 8 years – at least – in old wood, slowly gaining colour and intensity. The nuttiness is more walnut and hazelnut than brazil nut and the old stairway dust and cold scrubbed floorboard is more fino than amontillado, and as for the scent of mint leaves and orange peel – well, I'm not used to that in an amontillado, but perhaps that's the new mark of Tio Diego.

Fino Inocente, Valdespino, 18% abv
Martinez Wines, Moreno Wine, £11.99, Lea & Sandeman, £12.95

I don't like using phrases like 'icon wine'. But sometimes I feel a wine has earned the status by consistently reaching for the ultimate expression of style and character. Valdespino Inocente achieved this status, with stellar wines from its ancient bodega in the backstreets of Jerez. Then, to my horror, the bodega and its vast store of maturing sherry was shifted – 'to some new place on the other side of the ringroad' is how one sherry friend put it. And I do think the quality took a dip. But now it's back. And if you want to experience the ultimate fino sherry, once more Valdespino is the name to look for. Fino sherry is really the driest of dry wines when it's good. Yet there is a sweet core – or can there be? What sweetness can there be in the heart of dryness? Can you have 'fat-free' cream? When you're describing great dry sherry, every term you use seems to rebel against drinking pleasure, yet is crucial to it. This tastes of earth – summer earth, dried out after a brief summer shower. This tastes of dust – dust caught in a shaft of sunlight through the banisters of an old staircase. This tastes of an old chest of drawers, of old clean wool, pebbles, apple, cedar and orange, ether – yes, ether – a traditional doctor's surgery, an old, clean Victorian hospital ward. Formaldehyde, the bitter bark of medicinal trees. Hmm. Inocente's back – in all its paradoxical, confusing, inspiring glory.

Sweet Oloroso, La Copita (Emilio Lustau), 20% abv
Oddbins, £7.99

You'll do much better buying this sweet sherry than the ones that spend millions of pounds on advertising in the run-up to Christmas, or the gaudy brands in the supermarket half-price dump-bins. Sweet sherry can be lovely, but it needs to taste of sherry. This is rich and sweet but the sweetness is based on good old wine matured in big barrels, not just a squirt of sugar syrup. This tastes of spicy raisins, syrup of dark figs, dates and nuts, and you could drink it to warm yourself up on a cold winter's day, or with the slice of cake you guiltily eat by the fireside.

Amontillado Maribel, Sánchez Romate, 19% abv
The Wine Society, £7.50

I knew a lady called Maribel once. We sang ditties down by the lake… I'm not saying any more, but it was usually springtime, and this is more of a dry, dark sherry for winter evenings. Nutty, quite rich in a sugarless way, still tasting of the dry old wood in which it lay for years before the bottler called, and with a nip of acid to keep you awake in case the fire needs stoking.

Dry Amontillado Sherry, aged 12 years, Lustau/Sainsbury's Taste the Difference, 19% abv
Sainsbury's, £6.49/50cl

Amontillado has been given a bad name as a medium-sweet cupful of brown goo served to you by aunts, in-laws and vicars. Well, cheap amontillado is a bit like that. But real amontillado is a delight. For a start, it's dry, and chestnut in colour, and has a unique richness of buttered brazils and butter caramel, seasoned with other old brown sweet perfumes and flavours like brown manila envelopes, walnuts and dates. But above all it's the texture and flavour of butter caramel – but dry and sugarless as can be.

Dry Oloroso Sherry, aged 12 years, Lustau/Sainsbury's Taste the Difference, 20% abv
Sainsbury's, £6.49/50cl

Dry oloroso is rarely completely dry, but it should never be sugary, and should manage a dangerous, challenging high-wire act balancing richness and age of flavours with tongue-cleansing dryness. This has a real sense of rich old brown things placed silently in a line on a pantry table – a handful of hazelnuts and walnuts, a box of Medjool dates, dark figs in syrup, shrivelled raisins in a little pile – and behind all these, in the shadows, more secrets and magic buried in the sherry's heart.

Sweet Pedro Ximenez Sherry (pudding wine), aged 12 years, Williams & Humbert/ Sainsbury's Taste the Difference, 18% abv   Sainsbury's, £6.49/50cl

It's possible you will never have experienced any wine quite as overwhelmingly sweet as this. It's dark brown, and so viscous it hardly flows from the bottle. Essence of grape, essence of syrup, essence of every fruit that ever hung a day too long on the bough as the wasps swarmed and shouted to be the first to catch that teardrop of nectar as it appears by the stalk. You had your chance. You could have picked it yesterday. The wasps play fair. Until they see that liquid bud form and they pounce in a frenzied flailing hysteria to suck such sweet nectar. This sweet nectar.

Manzanilla (Williams & Humbert), 15% abv Marks & Spencer, £5.99

Manzanilla is the driest and the most savoury of sherry styles, coming from bodegas so close to the beach that you can sometimes smell the brine in the wine. This is very dry, lean, with some of the dust of the old banisters at the top of an empty house, a creamy sourness like bread dough risen and puffy, just before it's thrown into the oven, and a smooth austerity like pebbles on the beach. The apple core and hazelnut suggest a slight sweetness, but don't be fooled, there's none there.

Manzanilla (Bodegas Almirante), 15% abv Asda, £5.47

This has been very slightly softened at the edges, but the flavour is still good and it'll do an excellent job when it's nicely chilled down. It has the typical dry sherry sour edge that seems to blend so primly with the dust of the spinster's staircase. And it does have a soft core of hazelnut and the crust of freshly baked white bread.

PORT

1998 Graham's Quinta dos Malvedos Vintage Port, 20% abv
Sainsbury's, £29.99

When a vintage doesn't quite measure up to the gold standard, the best estates – quintas – often bottle a wine under their own label. Since vintage port is generally a blend of top estates' wines, you could thumb your nose at these 'single-quinta' wines. Or you could follow me and buy them, because they're cheaper, they mature quicker, and they give you a feel for a property, rather than a blend. Malvedos is Graham's best property, the backbone of their vintage port, so this is guaranteed to be classy, even though 1998 was a tricky vintage. It's beautifully scented, full of raspberry and loganberry fruit just gasping for the first opportunity to go deeper into the sweet delights of blackberry, cinnamon and clove spice, a very light dose of spirit and tannin, and an academic suggestion of library dust – a lovely wine.

2001 Taylor's Vargellas Vintage Port, 20% abv
Majestic, Oddbins, Tesco, Waitrose, £25–£30

Marvellous, indulgent version of the new style of gentler port. Vargellas has never been a dense, aggressive mouthful, but this is particularly smooth and chubby-cheeked, with spice and plush juicy fruit replacing some of the attack and power. The port is soft and sweet and veers between red and black, one moment red plum and red cherry, then loganberry and just the beginnings of blackberry.

1999 Warre's bottle-matured Late Bottled Vintage (unfiltered, bottled 2003) 20% abv
Waitrose, £19.99

This wine has given me so much pleasure over the years, and it has also provided me with so much ammunition. Late Bottled Vintage (LBV) has become a commercially-skewed way of talking about a wood-aged, tightly filtered wine that shippers will say has 'vintage' characteristics – but to be honest, they were stripped out by the filter machine. Vintage ports are not filtered. If you want vintage characteristics you must accept the nuisances of sediment. But there is a way to soften high-quality port, reduce but not eliminate its sediment, and have it at its peak of perfection at perhaps 10 years, rather than the 20 or so a full-blooded vintage would require. You leave it in barrel for 4 years (vintage port only spends 2 years in barrel). Barrel aging softens and lightens the wine and throws off a lot of sediment. Then you bottle it, unfiltered, preserving all the perfume and fruit and texture. And you get a wonderfully rich, complex and mature wine – far more interesting than the big-brand filtered LBVs and far more approachable than the brooding, beetle-browed Vintage ports. This is midweight, with a lovely gentle texture – just a little muscular tannin – but mostly delightful loganberry and blackberry fruit, scented with rosehip and kitchen spice.

Fonseca Crusted Port (bottled 2004), 20% abv
Majestic, £15.99

Fonseca ports are renowned for having lovely rich, ripe fruit at every level.
This Crusted doesn't disappoint. It's full of sweet loganberry fruit that's eternally punching above
its weight and reaching out longingly towards blackberry. It's not just fruit – there's a nice spicy scent,
there's an undertow of metallic minerality and there's a slight bitterness which is hardly about wine at all,
and more about the pips in your teeth when you're eating raspberries.

Graham's Crusted Port (bottled 2002), 20% abv
Wine Rack, £15.99

Crusted port is nearly but not quite vintage style, for a far lower price. It's a blend of wines from two or three
years, not quite top level, but full of character. It's bottled after quite a short time in barrel, then kept for
at least three years before sale (this one has been kept for seven years). The result is powerful, with rich
flavours of plum, blackberry and cherry, and there's some peppery bite and youthful attack to balance
out the lush, deep, dark, scented wine.

Terra Prima Port (organic), Fonseca, 20% abv
Waitrose, £14.99

Now this is modern port. For a start, it's organic. Organic has never been a buzzword in the Douro, where
peasant proprietors and port producers more often merely talk the language of alcoholic degree and tonnes
per hectare. Well, if the flavour of this is anything to go by, organic might now mean something in the
Douro: not only is the fruit plump and fresh – cherry and plums and raspberries, but also
plump black grapes – but there's also floral scent, and a very sophisticated
sheen of new leather and polished wood. And almost no tannin and spirit to
interfere. Very modern.

Sainsbury's 10 Year Old Tawny Port (Symington Family Estates), 20% abv
Sainsbury's, £11.49

I tasted quite a lot of tawnies this year and came to the conclusion most of them had been made by rugby players. They were too heavy, too rich, too dark in colour and muscular in frame. Tawny port, aged – for 10 years or maybe twice that – in old oak barrels, is basically an elegant drink, one that flows silkily across your palate; it shouldn't bludgeon your sensibilities with power and attitude. So I've just chosen one – though even this is on the full side. But it does have a nice chestnut amber colour with just a hint of blush, and it does have the warm sweetness of raisins and dates and fruit cake, and the sweet scent of manila envelopes, as well as a nuttiness that verges on the savouriness of salted almonds.

Pink Port, 19% abv
Marks & Spencer, £7.99

And they mean pink. This is shocking, eye-popping, day-glo pink, party pink, candyfloss pink. It's not serious or complicated, it's got a really fresh sweetness based on apple and peach, scented with rosehip and a little peppercorn that just says – fun. Have it.

Ruby Port (Symington Family Estates), 19% abv
Asda, £5.54

Good, gutsy, fruity stuff. This is much better than the dirt cheap grocers' port you'd have to mix with lemonade and Ribena to make it drinkable. This is proper, serious port. It's got deep, quite mature plum and blackberry fruit, some clove and cinnamon spice and enough class for you to confidently serve it at the end of a meal. It's made by top producers Symington, who make the wines like Graham's and Warre's, and this tastes as though they've included some superior off-cuts in the blend.

• Waitrose Ruby and Sainsbury's Ruby are much the same price and also good.

Storing, serving and tasting

Wine is all about enjoyment, so don't let anyone make you anxious about opening, serving, tasting and storing it. Here are some tips to help you enjoy your wine all the more.

The corkscrew

The first step in tasting any wine is to extract the cork. Look for a corkscrew with an open spiral and a comfortable handle. The Screwpull brand is far and away the best, with a high-quality open spiral. 'Waiter's friend' corkscrews – the type you see used in restaurants – are good too, once you get the knack.

Corkscrews with a solid core that looks like a giant woodscrew tend to mash up delicate corks or get stuck in tough ones. And try to avoid those 'butterfly' corkscrews with the twin lever arms and a bottle opener on the end; they tend to leave cork crumbs floating in the wine.

Corks

Don't be a cork snob. The only requirements for the seal on a bottle of wine are that it should be hygienic, airtight, long-lasting and removable. Real cork is environmentally friendly, but is prone to shrinkage and infection, which can taint the wine. Synthetic closures modelled on the traditional cork are common in budget wines, but the largest increase has been in the use of screwcaps, or Stelvin closures, which are now appearing on some very classy wines, especially in Australia and New Zealand, South Africa and South America.

Decanting

Transferring wine to a decanter brings it into contact with oxygen, which can open up the flavours. You don't need to do this ages before serving and you don't need a special decanter: a glass jug is just as good. And there's no reason why you shouldn't decant the wine to aerate it, then pour it back into its bottle to serve it.

Mature red wine is likely to contain sediment and needs careful handling. Stand the bottle upright for a day or two to let the sediment fall to the bottom. Open the wine carefully, and place a torch or candle beside the decanter. As you pour, stand so that you can see the light shining through the neck of the bottle. Pour the wine into the decanter in one steady motion and stop when you see the sediment reaching the neck of the bottle.

Temperature

The temperature of wine has a bearing on its flavour. Heavy reds are happy at room temperature, but the lighter the wine the cooler it should be. I'd serve Burgundy and other Pinot Noir reds at cool larder temperature. Juicy, fruity young reds, such as wines from the Loire Valley, are refreshing served lightly chilled.

Chilling white wines makes them taste fresher, but also subdues flavours, so bear this in mind if you're splashing out on a top-quality white – don't keep it in the fridge too long. Sparkling wines, however, must be well chilled to avoid exploding corks and fountains of foam.

For quick chilling, fill a bucket with ice and cold water, plus a few spoonfuls of salt if you're in a real hurry. This is much more effective than ice on its own. If the wine is already cool, a vacuum-walled cooler will maintain the temperature.

The wine glass

The ideal wine glass is a fairly large tulip shape, made of fine, clear glass, with a slender stem. This shape helps to concentrate the aromas of the wine and to show off its colours and texture. For sparkling wine choose a tall, slender glass, as it helps the bubbles to last longer.

Look after your glasses carefully. Detergent residues or grease can affect the flavour of any wine and reduce the bubbliness of sparkling wine. Ideally, wash glasses in very hot water and don't use detergent at all. Rinse glasses thoroughly and allow them to air-dry. Store wine glasses upright to avoid trapping stale odours.

Keeping opened bottles

Exposure to oxygen causes wine to deteriorate. Once opened, it will last fairly well for a couple of days if you just push the cork back in and stick the bottle in the fridge, but you can also buy a range of effective devices to help keep oxygen at bay. Vacuvin uses a rubber stopper and a vacuum pump to remove air from the bottle. Others inject inert gas into the bottle to shield the wine from the ravages of oxidation.

Laying down wine

The longer you intend to keep wine before you drink it, the more important it is to store it with care. If you haven't got a cellar, find a nook – under the stairs, a built-in cupboard or a disused fireplace – that is cool, relatively dark and vibration-free, in which you can store the bottles on their sides to keep the corks moist (if a cork dries out it will let air in and spoil the wine).

Wine should be kept cool – around 10–15°C/50–55°F. It is also important to avoid sudden temperature changes or extremes: a windowless garage or outhouse may be cool in summer but may freeze in winter. Exposure to light can ruin wine, but dark bottles go some way to protecting it from light.

How to taste wine

If you just knock your wine back like a cold beer, you'll be missing most of whatever flavour it has to offer. Take a bit of time to pay attention to what you're tasting and I guarantee you'll enjoy the wine more.

Read the label

There's no law that says you have to make life hard for yourself when tasting wine. So have a look at what you're drinking and read the notes on the back label if there is one. The label will tell you the vintage, the region and/or the grape variety, the producer and the alcohol level.

Look at the wine

Pour the wine into a glass so it is a third full and tilt it against a white background so you can enjoy the range of colours in the wine. Is it dark or light? Is it viscous or watery? As you gain experience, the look of the wine will tell you one or two things about the age and the likely flavour and weight of the wine. As a wine ages, whites lose their springtime greenness and gather deeper, golden hues, whereas red wines trade the purple of youth for a paler brick red.

Swirl and sniff

Give the glass a vigorous swirl to wake up the aromas in the wine, stick your nose in and inhale gently. This is where you'll be hit by the amazing range of smells a wine can produce. Interpret them in any way that means something to you personally: it's only by reacting honestly to the taste and smell of a wine that you can build up a memory bank of flavours against which to judge future wines.

Take a sip

At last! It's time to drink the wine. So take a decent-sized slurp – enough to fill your mouth about a third full. The tongue can detect only very basic flavour elements: sweetness at the tip, acidity at the sides and bitterness at the back. The real business of tasting goes on in a cavity at the back of the mouth that is really part of the nose. The idea is to get the fumes from the wine to rise up into this nasal cavity. Note the toughness, acidity and sweetness of the wine, then suck some air through the wine to help the flavours on their way. Gently 'chew' the wine and let it coat your tongue, teeth, cheeks and gums. Jot down a few notes as you form your opinion and then make the final decision... Do you like it or don't you?

Swallow or spit it out

If you are tasting a lot of wines, you will have to spit as you go if you want to remain upright and retain your judgement. Otherwise, go ahead and swallow and enjoy the lovely aftertaste of the wine.

Wine faults

If you order wine in a restaurant and you find one of these faults you are entitled to a replacement. Many retailers will also replace a faulty bottle if you return it the day after you open it, with your receipt. Sometimes faults affect random bottles, others may ruin a whole case of wine.

- Cork taint – a horrible musty, mouldy smell indicates 'corked' wine, caused by a contaminated cork.
- Volatile acidity – pronounced vinegary or acetone smells.
- Oxidation – sherry-like smells are not appropriate in red and white wines.
- Hydrogen sulphide – 'rotten eggs' smell.

Watchpoints

- Sediment in red wines makes for a gritty, woody mouthful. To avoid this, either decant the wine or simply pour it gently, leaving the last few centilitres of wine in the bottle.
- White crystals, or tartrates, on the cork or at the bottom of bottles of white wine are both harmless and flavourless.
- Sticky bottle neck – if wine has seeped past the cork it probably hasn't been very well kept and air might have got in. This may mean oxidized wine.
- Excess sulphur dioxide is sometimes noticeable as a smell of a recently struck match; it should dissipate after a few minutes.

Wine style guide

When faced with a shelf – or a screen – packed with wines from around the world, where do you start? Well, if you're after a particular flavour, my guide to wine styles will point you in the right direction.

White wines
Bone-dry, neutral whites

Neutral wines exist for the sake of seafood or to avoid interrupting you while you're eating. It's a question of balance, rather than aromas and flavours, but there will be a bit of lemon, yeast and a mineral thrill in a good Muscadet *sur lie* or a proper Chablis. Loads of Italian whites do the same thing, but Italy is increasingly picking up on the global shift towards fruit flavours and maybe some oak. Basic, cheap South African whites are often a good bet if you want something thirst-quenching and easy to drink. Colombard and Chenin are fairly neutral grape varieties widely used in South Africa, often producing appley flavours, and better examples add a lick of honey.

- Muscadet
- Chenin Blanc and Colombard – from the Loire Valley, South-West France, Australia, California or South Africa
- Basic white Bordeaux and Entre-Deux-Mers
- Chablis
- Pinot Grigio

Green, tangy whites

For nerve-tingling refreshment, Sauvignon Blanc is the classic grape, full of fresh grass, gooseberry and nettle flavours. I always used to go for New Zealand versions, but I'm now more inclined to reach for an inexpensive bottle from Chile, South Africa or Hungary. Or even a simple white Bordeaux, because suddenly

Bordeaux Sauvignon is buzzing with life. Most Sancerre and the other Loire Sauvignons are overpriced. Austria's Grüner Veltliner has a peppery freshness. From north-west Iberia, Galicia's Albariño grape has a stony, mineral lemon zest sharpness; the same grape is used in Portugal, for Vinho Verde. Alternatively, look at Riesling: Australia serves it up with aggressive lime and mineral flavours, and New Zealand and Chile give milder versions of the same style. Alsace Riesling is lemony and dry, while German Rieslings go from bone-dry to intensely sweet, with the tangiest, zestiest, coming from the Mosel Valley.

- Sauvignon Blanc – from New Zealand, Chile, Hungary, South Africa, or Bordeaux
- Loire Valley Sauvignons such as Sancerre and Pouilly-Fumé
- Riesling – from Australia, Austria, Chile, Germany, New Zealand, or Alsace in France
- Austrian Grüner Veltliner
- Vinho Verde from Portugal and Albariño from north-west Spain

Intense, nutty whites

The best white Burgundy from the Côte d'Or cannot be bettered for its combination of soft nut and oatmeal flavours, subtle, buttery oak and firm, dry structure. Prices are often hair-raising and the cheaper wines rarely offer much Burgundy style. For around £8–10 your best bet is oaked Chardonnay from an innovative Spanish region such as Somontano or Navarra. You'll get a nutty, creamy taste and nectarine fruit with good oak-aged white Bordeaux or traditional white Rioja. Top Chardonnays from New World countries – and Italy for that matter – can emulate Burgundy, but once again we're looking at serious prices.

- White Burgundy – including Meursault, Pouilly-Fuissé, Chassagne-Montrachet, Puligny-Montrachet
- White Bordeaux – including Pessac-Léognan, Graves
- White Rioja
- Chardonnay from New Zealand and Oregon – and top examples from Australia, California and South Africa

Ripe, toasty whites

Aussie Chardonnay conquered the world with its upfront flavours of peaches, apricots and melons, usually spiced up by the vanilla, toast and butterscotch richness of new oak. This winning style has now become a standard-issue flavour produced by all sorts of countries, though I still love the original. You'll need to spend a bit more than a fiver nowadays if you want something to relish beyond the first glass. Oaked Australian Semillon can also give rich, ripe fruit flavours, as can oaked Chenin Blanc from New Zealand and South Africa. If you see the words 'unoaked' or 'cool-climate' on an Aussie bottle, expect an altogether leaner drink.

- Chardonnay: from Australia, Chile, California, South Africa
- Oak-aged Chenin Blanc from New Zealand and South Africa
- Australian Semillon

Aromatic whites

Alsace has always been a plentiful source of perfumed, dry or off-dry whites: Gewurztraminer with its rose and lychee scent or Muscat with its floral, hothouse grape perfume. A few producers in New Zealand, Australia, Chile and South Africa are having some success with these grapes. Floral, apricotty Viognier, traditionally the grape of Condrieu in the northern Rhône, now appears in vins de pays from all over southern France and also from California and Australia. Condrieu is expensive (£20 will get you entry-level stuff and no guarantee that it will be fragrant); vin de pays wines start at around £5 and are just as patchy. For aroma on a budget grab some Hungarian Irsai Olivér or Argentinian Torrontés. English white wines often have a fresh, floral hedgerow scent – the Bacchus grape is one of the leaders of this style.

- Alsace whites, especially Gewurztraminer and Muscat
- Gewürztraminer from Austria, Chile, Germany, New Zealand and cooler regions of Australia
- Condrieu, from the Rhône Valley in France
- Viognier from southern France, Argentina, Australia, California, Chile
- English white wines
- Irsai Olivér from Hungary
- Torrontés from Argentina

Golden, sweet whites

Good sweet wines are difficult to make and therefore expensive: prices for Sauternes and Barsac (from Bordeaux) can go through the roof, but near-neighbours Monbazillac, Loupiac, Saussignac and Ste-Croix-du-Mont are more affordable. Sweet Loire wines such as Quarts de Chaume, Bonnezeaux and some Vouvrays have a quince aroma and a fresh acidity that can keep them lively for decades, as do sweet Rieslings, such as Alsace Vendange Tardive, German and Austrian Beerenauslese (BA), Trockenbeeren-auslese (TBA) and Eiswein. Canadian icewine is quite rare over here, but we're seeing more of Hungary's Tokaji, with its sweet-sour, marmalade flavours.

- Sauternes, Barsac, Loupiac, Sainte-Croix-du-Mont
- Monbazillac, Saussignac, Jurançon and Pacherenc du Vic Bilh from South-West France
- Loire sweet whites such as Bonnezeaux, Quarts de Chaume and Vouvray moelleux
- Auslese, Beerenauslese and Trockenbeerenauslese from Germany and Austria
- Eiswein from Germany, icewine from Canada
- Botrytis Semillon, Riesling or Gewürztraminer from Australia

Red wines

Juicy, fruity reds

The definitive modern style for easy-going reds. Tasty, refreshing and delicious with or without food, they pack in loads of crunchy fruit while minimizing the tough, gum-drying tannins that characterize most traditional red wine styles. Beaujolais (made from the Gamay grape) is the prototype – and if you're distinctly underwhelmed by the very mention of the word 'Beaujolais', remember that the delightfully named Fleurie, St-Amour and Chiroubles also come from the Beaujolais region. Loire reds such as Chinon and Saumur (made from Cabernet Franc) pack in the fresh raspberries. Italy's Bardolino is light and refreshing, as is young Valpolicella. Nowadays, hi-tech producers all over the world are working the magic with a whole host of grape varieties. Carmenère, Malbec and Merlot are always good bets, and Grenache/Garnacha and Tempranillo usually come up with the goods. Italian grapes like Bonarda, Barbera and Sangiovese seem to double in succulence under Argentina's blazing sun. And at around £6–7 even Cabernet Sauvignon – if it's from somewhere warm like Australia, South America, South Africa or Spain – or a vin de pays Syrah from southern France, will emphasize the fruit and hold back on the tannin.

- Beaujolais – including Brouilly, Chiroubles, Fleurie, Juliénas, Moulin-à-Vent, St-Amour. Also wines made from the Gamay grape in other parts of France
- Loire reds: Chinon, Saumur, Saumur-Champigny – and, if you're lucky, Bourgueuil, Cheverny and St-Nicolas de Bourgueil
- Grenache (from France) and Garnacha (from Spain)
- Carmenère from Chile
- Basic Merlot from just about anywhere
- Inexpensive Argentinian reds, especially Bonarda, but also Sangiovese and Tempranillo

Silky, strawberryish reds

Here we're looking for some special qualities, specifically a gorgeously smooth texture and a heavenly fragrance of strawberries, raspberries or cherries. We're looking for soft, decadent, seductive wines.

One grape – Pinot Noir – and one region – Burgundy – stand out, but prices are high to astronomical. Good red Burgundy is addictively hedonistic and all sorts of strange decaying aromas start to hover around the strawberries as the wine ages. Pinot Noirs from New Zealand, California, Oregon and, increasingly, Australia come close, but they're expensive, too; Chilean Pinots are far more affordable. You can get that strawberry perfume (though not the silky texture) from other grapes in Spain's Navarra, Rioja and up-coming regions like La Mancha and Murcia. Southern Rhône blends can deliver if you look for fairly light examples of Côtes du Rhône-Villages or Costières de Nîmes.

- Red Burgundy – including Chassagne-Montrachet, Beaune, Givry, Nuits-St-Georges, Pommard
- Pinot Noir from Australia, California, Chile, New Zealand, Oregon
- Spanish reds from Rioja, Navarra, La Mancha and Valdepeñas, especially with Tempranillo as the main grape
- Red blends from the southern Rhône Valley, such as Costières de Nîmes, Côtes du Rhône-Villages, Gigondas
- Australian Grenache

Intense, blackcurranty reds

Firm, intense wines which often only reveal their softer side with a bit of age; Cabernet Sauvignon is the grape, on its own or blended with Merlot or other varieties. Bordeaux is the classic region but there are far too many overpriced underachievers there. And Cabernet's image has changed. You can still choose the austere, tannic style, in theory aging to a heavenly cassis and cedar maturity, but most of the world is taking a fruitier blackcurrant-and-mint approach. Chile does the fruity style par excellence. New Zealand can deliver Bordeaux-like flavours, but in a faster-maturing wine. Australia often adds a medicinal eucalyptus twist or a dollop of blackcurrant jam. Argentina and South Africa are making their mark too. In Spain, Ribera del Duero can also come up with blackcurrant flavours.

- Bordeaux reds such as Côtes de Castillon, St-Émilion, Pomerol
- Cabernet Sauvignon from just about anywhere
- Cabernet Sauvignon-Merlot blends

Spicy, warm-hearted reds

Australian Shiraz is the epitome of this rumbustious, riproaring style: dense, rich, chocolaty, sometimes with a twist of pepper, a whiff of smoke, or a slap of leather. But it's not alone. There are southern Italy's Primitivo and Nero d'Avola, California's Zinfandel, Mexico's Petite Sirah, Argentina's Malbec, South Africa's Pinotage, Toro from Spain and some magnificent Greek reds. In southern France the wines of the Languedoc often show this kind of warmth, roughed up with hillside herbs. And if you want your spice more serious, more smoky and minerally, go for the classic wines of the northern Rhône Valley.

- Australian Shiraz, as well as blends of Shiraz with Grenache and Mourvèdre/Mataro – and Durif
- Northern Rhône Syrah (Cornas, Côte-Rôtie, Hermitage, St-Joseph) and southern Rhône blends such as Châteauneuf-du-Pape
- Southern French reds, such as Corbières, Coteaux du Languedoc, Côtes du Roussillon, Faugères, Fitou, Minervois
- Italian reds such as Primitivo, Aglianico, Negroamaro and Nero d'Avola
- Zinfandel and Petite Sirah reds
- Argentinian Malbec

Mouthwatering, sweet-sour reds

Sounds weird? This style is primarily the preserve of Italy, and it's all about food: the rasp of sourness cuts through rich, meaty food, with a lip-smacking tingle that works equally well with pizza or tomato-based pasta dishes. But there's fruit in there too – cherries and plums – plus raisiny sweetness and a herby bite. The wines are now better made than ever, with more seductive fruit, but holding on to those fascinating flavours. All sorts of native Italian grape varieties deliver this delicious sour-cherries taste: Sangiovese (the classic red grape of Tuscany), Nebbiolo (from Piedmont), Barbera, Dolcetto, Teroldego, Sagrantino... You'll have to shell out up to a tenner for decent Chianti, more for Piedmont wines (especially Barolo and Barbaresco, so try Langhe instead). Valpolicella can be very good, but choose with care. Portugal reveals something of the same character in its reds.

- Chianti, plus other wines made from the Sangiovese grape
- Barolo, Barbaresco and other wines made from the Nebbiolo grape
- Valpolicella Classico, Amarone della Valpolicella
- Southern Italian reds
- Touriga Nacional and other Portuguese reds

Delicate (and not-so-delicate) rosé

Dry rosé can be wonderful, with flavours of strawberries and maybe raspberries and rosehips, cherries, apples and herbs, too. Look for wines made from sturdy grapes like Cabernet, Syrah or Merlot, or go for Grenache/Garnacha or Tempranillo from Spain and the Rhône Valley. South America is a good bet for flavoursome, fruit-forward pink wine. *See pages 102–7 for my top pinks this year.*

Drink organic – or even biodynamic

- The widely discussed benefits of organic farming – respect for the environment, minimal chemical residues in our food and drink – apply to grapes as much as to any other produce. Full-blown organic viticulture forbids the use of synthetic fertilizers, herbicides or fungicides; instead, cover crops and companion planting encourage biodiversity and natural predators to keep the soil and vines healthy. Warm, dry climates like the South of France, Chile and South Africa have the advantage of rarely suffering from the damp that can cause rot, mildew and other problems – we should be seeing more organic wines from these regions. Organic wines from European countries are often labelled 'Biologique', or simply 'Bio'.
- Biodynamic viticulture takes working with nature one stage further: work in the vineyard is planned in accordance with the movements of the planets, moon, sun and cosmic forces to achieve health and balance in the soil and in the vine. Vines are treated with infusions of mineral, animal and plant materials, applied in homeopathic quantities, with some astonishing results.
- If you want to know more, the best companies to contact are Vinceremos and Vintage Roots (see pages 186–7).

Sparkling wines

Champagne can be the finest sparkling wine on the planet, but fizz made by the traditional Champagne method in Australia, New Zealand or California – often using the same grape varieties – is often just as good and cheaper. It might be a little more fruity, where Champagne concentrates on bready, yeasty or nutty aromas, but a few are dead ringers for the classic style. Fizz is also made in other parts of France: Crémant de Bourgogne is one of the best. England is beginning to show its potential. Italy's Prosecco is soft and delicately scented. Spain's Cava is perfect party fizz available at bargain basement prices in all the big supermarkets.

• Champagne
• Traditional method fizz made from Chardonnay, Pinot Noir and Pinot Meunier grapes grown in Australia, California, England, New Zealand, South Africa
• Crémant de Bourgogne, Crémant de Loire, Crémant de Jura, Crémant d'Alsace, Blanquette de Limoux
• Cava
• Prosecco
• Sekt is Germany's sparkling wine, and is occasionally 100 per cent Riesling
• Lambrusco from Italy is gently sparkling and usually red
• Sparkling Shiraz – an Aussie speciality – will make a splash at a wild party

Fortified wines

Tangy, appetizing fortified wines

To set your taste buds tingling, fino and manzanilla sherries are pale, perfumed, bone dry and bracingly tangy. True amontillado, dark and nutty, is also dry. Dry oloroso adds deep, raisiny flavours. Palo cortado falls between amontillado and oloroso; manzanilla pasada is an older, nuttier manzanilla. The driest style of Madeira, Sercial, is steely and smoky; Verdelho Madeira is a bit fuller and richer, but still tangy and dry.

- Manzanilla and fino sherry
- Dry amontillado, palo cortado and dry oloroso sherry
- Sercial and Verdelho Madeira

Rich, warming fortified wines

Raisins and brown sugar, dried figs and caramelized nuts – do you like the sound of that? Port is the classic dark sweet wine, and it comes in several styles, from basic ruby, to tawny, matured in cask for 10 years or more, to vintage, which matures to mellowness in the bottle. The Portuguese island of Madeira produces fortified wines with rich brown smoky flavours and a startling bite of acidity: the sweet styles to look for are Bual and Malmsey. Decent sweet sherries are rare; oloroso dulce is a style with stunningly concentrated flavours. In southern France, Banyuls and Maury are deeply fruity fortified wines. Marsala, from Sicily, has rich brown sugar flavours with a refreshing sliver of acidity. The versatile Muscat grape makes luscious golden wines all around the Mediterranean, but also pops up in orange, black, and the gloriously rich, treacly brown versions that Australia does superbly.

- Port
- Bual and Malmsey Madeira
- Marsala
- Rich, sweet sherry styles include Pedro Ximénez, oloroso dulce
- Vins doux naturels from southern France: Banyuls, Maury
- Fortified (liqueur) Muscat 'stickies' from Australia

Buying wine for the long term

Most of this book is about wines to drink more or less immediately – that's how modern wines are made, and that's what you'll find in most high street retail outlets. If you're looking for a mature vintage of a great wine that's ready to drink – or are prepared to wait 10 years or more for a great vintage to reach its peak – specialist wine merchants will be able to help; the internet's another good place to look for mature wines. Here's my beginners' guide to buying wine for drinking over the longer term.

Auctions

A wine sale catalogue from one of the UK's auction houses will have wine enthusiasts drooling over names they certainly don't see every day. Better still, the lots are often of mature vintages that are ready to drink. Before you go, find out all you can about the producer and vintages described in the catalogue. My annually updated *Pocket Wine Book* is a good place to start, or *Michael Broadbent's Vintage Wines* for old and rare wines; the national wine magazines (*Decanter*, *Wine & Spirit*) run regular features on wine regions and their vintages. You can also learn a lot from tutored tastings – especially 'vertical' tastings, which compare different vintages. This is important – some merchants take the opportunity to clear inferior vintages at auction.

The drawbacks? You have no guarantee that the wine has been well stored, and if it's faulty you have little chance of redress. As prices of the most sought-after wines have soared, so it has become profitable either to forge the bottles and their contents or to try to pass off stock that is clearly out of condition. But for expensive and mature wines, I have to say that the top auction houses make a considerable effort to check the provenance and integrity of the wines. Don't forget that there will usually be a commission or buyers' premium to pay, so check out the small print in the sale catalogue. Online wine auctions have similar pros and cons.

If you've never bought wine at an auction before, a good place to start would be a local auctioneer such as Straker Chadwick in Abergavenny (tel: 01873 852624, www.strakerchadwick.co.uk) or Morphets in Harrogate (tel: 01423 530030, www.morphets.co.uk); they're less intimidating than the famous London houses of Christie's and Sotheby's and you may come away with some really exciting wine.

Buying en primeur

En primeur is a French term for wine which is sold before it is bottled, sometimes referred to as a 'future'. In the spring after the vintage, the Bordeaux châteaux – and a few other wine-producing regions – hold tastings of barrel samples for members of the international wine trade. The châteaux then offer a proportion of their production to the wine merchants (*négociants*) in Bordeaux, who in turn offer it to wine merchants around the world at an opening price.

The advantage to the châteaux is that their capital is not tied up in expensive stock for the next year or two, until the wines are bottled and ready to ship. Traditionally merchants would buy en primeur for stock to be sold later at a higher price, while offering their customers the chance to take advantage of the opening prices as well. The idea of private individuals investing rather than institutions took off with a series of good Bordeaux vintages in the 1980s; it's got ever more hectic since then.

Wine for the future

There is a lot to be said for buying en primeur. For one thing, in a great vintage you may be able to find the finest and rarest wines far more cheaply than they will ever appear again. Every classic vintage in Bordeaux opens at a higher and higher price, but that price never drops, and so the top wines increase in value, whatever price they start at. Equally, when a wine – even a relatively inexpensive one – is made in very limited quantities, buying en primeur may be practically your only chance of getting hold of it.

In the past, British wine merchants and their privileged customers were able to 'buy double what you want, sell half for double what you paid, and drink for free', but as the market has opened up to people more interested in making a quick buck than drinking fine wine, the whole process has become more risky.

Another potential hazard is that a tasting assessment is difficult at an early date. There is a well-founded suspicion that many barrel samples are doctored (legally) to appeal to the most powerful consumer critics, in particular the American Robert Parker and the *Wine Spectator* magazine. The wine that is finally bottled may or may not bear a resemblance to what was tasted in the spring following the vintage. In any case, most serious red wines are in a difficult stage of their evolution in the spring, and with the best will in the world it is possible to get one's evaluation wrong. However, the aforementioned Americans, and magazines like *Decanter* and *Wine & Spirit*, will do their best to offer you accurate judgements on the newly offered wines, and most merchants who make a primeur offer also write a good assessment of the wines. You will find that many of them quote the Parker or *Wine Spectator* marks. Anything over 90 out of 100 risks being hyped and hiked in price. Many of the best bargains get marks between 85 and 89, since the 90+ marks are generally awarded for power rather than subtlety. Consideration can be given to the producer's reputation for consistency and to the general vintage assessment for the region.

Prices can go down as well as up. They may not increase significantly for some years after the campaign.

Some popular vintages are offered at ridiculously high prices – some unpopular ones too. It's only about twice a decade that the combination of high quality and fair prices offers the private buyer a chance of a good, guaranteed profit. Interestingly, if one highly-touted vintage is followed by another, the prices for the second one often have to fall because the market simply will not accept two inflated price structures in a row. Recent Bordeaux examples of this are the excellent 1990 after the much hyped 1989 and the potentially fine 2001 after the understandably hyped 2000.

Bordeaux vintage update

The past 12 months have been chaotic in the Bordeaux fine wine market. Prices for the most sought-after wines slumped by 40% around the end of 2008 and are still recovering through 2009. But the wines that suffered most from this see-saw were a tiny number of trendy properties from the sexy vintages: obviously 2005, just about the most hyped vintage ever, but also the opulent and occasionally corpulent 2003 and the millennium 2000. Yet the rest – the wines that you and I might drink – never got too expensive in the first place, and didn't suffer much from the credit bust. Best of these are the ridiculously underrated 2004s; these classic Bordeaux are today's best buy. You can pick up less fêted 2005s – top cru bourgeois or lower-ranked Classed Growths – from as little as £20–30 a bottle. A First Growth will cost more like £800–1000 a bottle! 2006 and 2007 were expensive to start with and, although they're perfectly nice wines, they won't increase in value for some years yet.

2008 is more interesting. There are some beautiful wines, and many prices dropped by perhaps half before Robert Parker suddenly woke up and decided he liked the wines. Top wines are now back to £300 a bottle, but there are many lovely lesser wines, scented and balanced, for more like £25.

Secure cellarage

Another worry is that the merchant you buy the wine from may not still be around to deliver it to you two years later. Buy from a well-established merchant you trust, with a solid trading base in other wines.

Once the wines are shipped you may want your merchant to store the wine for you; there is usually a small charge for this. If your merchant offers cellarage, you should insist that (1) you receive a stock certificate; (2) your wines are stored separately from the merchant's own stocks; and (3) your cases are identifiable as your property. All good merchants offer these safeguards as a minimum service.

Check the small print

Traditional wine merchants may quote prices exclusive of VAT and/or duty: wine may not be the bargain it first appears. A wine quoted en primeur is usually offered on an ex-cellars (EC) basis; the price excludes shipping, duties and taxes such as VAT. A price quoted in bond (IB) in the UK includes shipping, but excludes duties and taxes. Duty paid (DP) prices exclude VAT. You should check beforehand the exact terms of sale with your merchant, who will give you a projection of the final 'duty paid delivered' price.

Retailers' directory

All these retailers have been chosen on the basis of the quality and interest of their lists. If you want to find a local retailer, turn to the Who's Where directory on page 192. Case = 12 bottles

The following services are available where indicated:
C = cellarage G = glass hire/loan M = mail/online order T = tastings and talks

A & B Vintners

Little Tawsden, Spout Lane, Brenchley, Kent TN12 7AS (01892) 724977
fax (01892) 722673 e-mail info@abvintners.co.uk website www.abvintners.co.uk
hours Mon–Fri 9–6 cards MasterCard, Visa delivery 1–4 cases £10 + VAT within M25; £15 Home Counties; free for
5 cases or more within these areas; phone for information on other areas minimum order 1 mixed case
en primeur Burgundy, Languedoc, Rhône. C M T
✪ Specialists in Burgundy, the Rhône and southern France, with a string of top-quality domaines from all three regions.

Adnams

head office & mail order Sole Bay Brewery, Southwold, Suffolk IP18 6JW (01502) 727222
fax (01502) 727223 e-mail customerservices@adnams.co.uk website www.adnams.co.uk
shops ● Adnams Wine Shop, Pinkney's Lane, Southwold, Suffolk IP18 6EW ● Adnams Cellar & Kitchen Stores: 4 Drayman
Square, Southwold, Suffolk, IP18 6GB ● The Old School House, Park Road, Holkham, Wells-next-the-Sea, Norfolk NR23
1AB (01328) 711714 ● Station Road, Woodbridge, Suffolk IP12 4AU (01394) 386594 ● Bath Row Warehouse, St Mary's
Passage, Stamford, Lincolnshire PE9 2HG (01780) 753127 ● The Cardinal's Hat, 23 The Thoroughfare, Harleston, Norfolk
IP20 9AS (01379) 854788 ● 1 Market Street, Saffron Walden, Essex CB10 1JB (01799) 527281 ● 23a Lees Yard, Off Bull
Street, Holt, Norfolk NR25 6HS (01263) 715558 ● 73–75 High Street, Hadleigh, Suffolk IP7 5DY (01473) 827796
● 26 Hill Rise, Richmond-upon-Thames, Surrey TW10 6UA (020) 8940 8684
hours (Orderline) Mon–Fri 9–6.00; Cellar & Kitchen Store Southwold: Mon–Sat 9–6, Sun 10–4; Wine Shop Southwold:
Mon–Sat 9.30–5.30, Sun 10–4; Holkham, Woodbridge and Stamford: Mon–Sat 10–6, Sun 11–4; Harleston: Mon–Sat
10–6; Holt: Mon–Sat 9–6, Sun 11–4; Hadleigh and Saffron Walden: Mon–Sat 9–6; Richmond: Mon–Sat 9–6, Sun 11–5

cards Maestro, MasterCard, Visa, Delta discounts 5% for 3 cases or more, 10% for 5 cases or more delivery Free for orders over £125 in most of mainland UK, otherwise £7.50 en primeur Bordeaux, Burgundy, Chile, Rhône. G

○ *Extensive list of personality-packed wines from around the world, chosen by Adnams' enthusiastic team of buyers.*

Aldi Stores

Holly Lane, Atherstone CV9 2SQ; over 400 stores in the UK customer service 0844 406 8800 website www.aldi.co.uk hours Mon–Fri 9–8, Sat 8.30–8, Sun 10–4 (selected stores; check the website) cards Maestro, MasterCard, Visa, Solo.

○ *Decent everyday stuff from around the world, with lots of wines under £4.*

armit

5 Royalty Studios, 105 Lancaster Road, London W11 1QF (020) 7908 0600
fax (020) 7908 0601 e-mail info@armit.co.uk website www.armit.co.uk hours Mon–Fri 9–5.30 cards Maestro, MasterCard, Visa delivery Free for orders over £250, otherwise £15 delivery charge minimum order 1 case en primeur Bordeaux, Burgundy, Italy, Rhône, New World. C M T

○ *Particularly strong on wines to go with food – they supply some of the country's top restaurants.*

ASDA

head office Asda House, Southbank, Great Wilson Street, Leeds LS11 5AD (0113) 243 5435
fax (0113) 241 8666 customer service (0500) 100055; 329 stores website www.asda.co.uk
hours Selected stores open 24 hours, see local store for details cards Maestro, MasterCard, Visa.

○ *Large and increasingly exciting range of great-value wines at all price points, selected by Philippa Carr MW.*

AustralianWineCentre.co.uk

mail order/online PO Box 3854, Datchet, Slough SL3 3EN 0800 756 1141 fax (01753) 591369
email customerservice@AustralianWineCentre.co.uk website www.AustralianWineCentre.co.uk cards MasterCard, Visa delivery Free for orders over £100, otherwise £5 per order; UK mainland only minimum order 1 mixed case.

○ *The original Aussie specialist with some brilliant Australian wines.*

Averys Wine Merchants

4 High Street, Nailsea, Bristol BS48 1BT 0845 863 0995
fax (01275) 811101 e-mail sales@averys.com website www.averys.com

• Shop and Cellars, 9 Culver Street, Bristol BS1 5LD (0117) 921 4146 fax (0117) 922 6318
e-mail cellars@averys.com
hours Mon–Fri 8–8, Sat–Sun 9–6; Shop Mon–Sat 10–7 cards Maestro, MasterCard, Visa
delivery £6.99 per delivery address en primeur Bordeaux, Burgundy, Port, Rhône. C G M T
○ *A small but very respectable selection from just about everywhere in France, Italy and Spain, as well as some good stuff from New Zealand, Australia and Chile.*

Ballantynes Wine Merchants

211–217 Cathedral Road, Cardiff CF11 9PP (02920) 222202
fax (02920) 222112 e-mail richard@ballantynes.co.uk website www.ballantynes-direct.co.uk
hours Mon–Fri 9.30–6.30, Sat 9.30–5.30 cards Access, Maestro, MasterCard, Visa
discounts 8% per case for local delivery or collection delivery Free for orders over £100; otherwise £10.99
minimum order £50 (mail order) en primeur Bordeaux, Burgundy, Italy, Rhône. C G M T
○ *Most regions of France are well represented; Italy, Spain and Portugal look good; and Australia and New Zealand are particularly tempting.*

Balls Brothers

313 Cambridge Heath Road, London E2 9LQ (020) 7739 1642
fax 0870 243 9775 direct sales (020) 7739 1642 e-mail wine@ballsbrothers.co.uk
website www.ballsbrothers.co.uk hours Mon–Fri 9–5.30 cards AmEx, Maestro, MasterCard, Visa
delivery Free 1 case or more locally; £10 for 1 case or free for orders over £175 in England, Wales and Scottish Lowlands; islands and Scottish Highlands, phone for details. G M T
○ *French specialist – you'll find something of interest from most regions – with older vintages available. Spain and Australia are also very good. Many of the wines can be enjoyed in Balls Brothers' London wine bars and restaurants.*

H & H Bancroft Wines

mail order 1 China Wharf, 29 Mill Street, London SE1 2BQ (020) 7232 5440
fax (020) 7232 5451 e-mail sales@bancroftwines.com website www.bancroftwines.com hours Mon–Fri 9–5.30
cards Delta, Maestro, MasterCard, Visa discounts Negotiable delivery £15 for 1–2 cases in mainland UK; free 3 cases or more or for orders of £350 or more minimum order 1 mixed case en primeur Bordeaux, Burgundy, Rhône. C M T

The following services are available where indicated: **C** = cellarage **G** = glass hire/loan **M** = mail/online order **T** = tastings and talks

○ *Bancroft are UK agents for an impressive flotilla of French winemakers: Burgundy, Rhône, Loire and some interesting wines from southern France. There is plenty of New World, too, and even wines from Slovenia.*

Bat & Bottle

Unit 5, 19 Pillings Road, Oakham LE15 6QF (01572) 759735
e-mail ben@batwine.co.uk website www.batwine.co.uk hours Mon–Fri 10–4, Sat 9–2: ring or check website before visiting cards Maestro, MasterCard, Visa delivery Free for orders over £150. G M T
○ *Ben and Emma Robson specialize in Italy, and in characterful wines from small producers.*

Bennetts Fine Wines

High Street, Chipping Campden, Glos GL55 6AG (01386) 840392 fax (01386) 840974
e-mail enquiries@bennettsfinewines.com website www.bennettsfinewines.com hours Tues–Sat 9.30–6
cards Access, Maestro, MasterCard, Visa discounts On collected orders of 1 case or more delivery £6 per case, minimum charge £12, free for orders over £200 en primeur Burgundy, California, Rhône, New Zealand. G M T
○ *Reasonable prices for high-calibre producers – there's lots to choose from at around £10. Mainly from France and Italy, but some good German, Spanish and Portuguese wines, too.*

Berkmann Wine Cellars

10–12 Brewery Road, London N7 9NH (020) 7609 4711 fax (020) 7607 0018 e-mail orders@berkmann.co.uk
• Brunel Park, Vincients Road, Bumpers Farm, Chippenham, Wiltshire SN14 6NQ (01249) 463501
fax (01249) 463502 e-mail orders.chippenham@berkmann.co.uk
• Churchill Vintners, 401 Walsall Road, Perry Bar, Birmingham B42 1BT (0121) 356 8888
fax (0121) 356 1111 e-mail info@churchill-vintners.co.uk
• Coad Wine Cellars, 41b Valley Road, Plympton, Plymouth, Devon PL7 1RF (01752) 334970
fax (01752) 346540 e-mail orders.briancoad@berkmann.co.uk
• Pagendam Pratt Wine Cellars, 16 Marston Moor Business Park, Rudgate, Tockwith, North Yorkshire YO26 7QF
(01423) 357567 fax (01423) 357568 e-mail orders@pagendampratt.co.uk
website www.berkmann.co.uk hours Mon–Fri 9–5.30 cards Maestro, MasterCard, Visa
discounts £3 per unmixed case collected delivery Free for orders over £120 to UK mainland (excluding the Highlands)
minimum order 1 mixed case. C M
○ *UK agent for, among others, Antinori, Casa Lapostolle, Chapel Hill, Deutz, Duboeuf, Mastroberardino, Masi, Norton, Rioja Alta and Tasca d'Almerita. An incredibly diverse list, with some great Italian wines.*

Berry Bros. & Rudd

3 St James's Street, London SW1A 1EG 0870 900 4300
sales and services 0800 280 2440 (lines open Mon–Fri 9–6) fax 0800 280 2443
• Berrys' Factory Outlet, Hamilton Close, Houndmills, Basingstoke, Hampshire RG21 6YB 0870 900 4300
e-mail bbr@bbr.com website www.bbr.com hours St James's Street: Mon–Fri 10–6, Sat 10–5; Berrys' Factory Outlet:
Mon–Fri 10–6, Sat–Sun 10–4 cards AmEx, Diners, Maestro, MasterCard, Visa discounts Variable
delivery Free for orders of £200 or more, otherwise £10 en primeur Bordeaux, Burgundy, Rhône. C G M T
✪ *Classy and wide-ranging list. There's an emphasis on the classic regions of France. Berry's Own Selection is extensive,*
with wines made by world-class producers.

Bibendum Wine

mail order 113 Regents Park Road, London NW1 8UR (020) 7449 4120
fax (020) 7449 4121 e-mail sales@bibendum-wine.co.uk website www.bibendum-wine.co.uk
hours Mon–Fri 9–6 cards Maestro, MasterCard, Visa delivery Free throughout mainland UK for orders over £250,
otherwise £15 en primeur Bordeaux, Burgundy, New World, Rhône, Port. M T
✪ *Equally strong in the Old World and the New: Huet in Vouvray and Lageder in Alto Adige are matched by d'Arenberg*
and Katnook from Australia and Catena Zapata from Argentina.

Big Red Wine Company

mail order Barton Coach House, The Street, Barton Mills, Suffolk IP28 6AA (01638) 510803
e-mail sales@bigredwine.co.uk website www.bigredwine.co.uk hours Mon–Sat 9–6
cards AmEx, Delta, Maestro, MasterCard, Visa, PayPal discounts 5–15% for Wine Club members; negotiable for large
orders delivery £7 per consignment for orders under £150, £10 for orders under £50, UK mainland
en primeur Bordeaux, Rhône. C G M T
✪ *Intelligently chosen, reliably individualistic wines from good estates in France, Italy and Spain. A list worth reading,*
full of information and provocative opinion – and they're not overcharging.

Booths

central office Longridge Road, Ribbleton, Preston PR2 5BX (01772) 693800; 26 stores across the North of England
fax (01772) 693893 website www.everywine.co.uk hours Office: Mon–Fri 8.30–5; shop hours vary
cards AmEx, Electron, Maestro, MasterCard, Solo, Visa discounts 5% off any 6 bottles. T

✪ *A list for any merchant to be proud of, never mind a supermarket. There's plenty around £5, but if you're prepared to hand over £7–9 you'll find some really interesting stuff.*

Bordeaux Index

mail order/online 10 Hatton Garden, London EC1N 8AH (020) 7269 0700
fax (020) 7269 0701 e-mail sales@bordeauxindex.com website www.bordeauxindex.com hours Mon–Fri 8.30–6
cards AmEx, Maestro, MasterCard, Visa, JCB (transaction fees apply) delivery (Private sales only) free for orders over
£2000 UK mainland; others at cost minimum order £500 en primeur Bordeaux, Burgundy, Rhône, Italy. C T
✪ *Extensive list of fine wines, including older vintages, focused on the classic regions of France and Italy, but with interesting stuff from elsewhere.*

Budgens Stores

head office Musgrave House, Widewater Place, Moorhall Road, Harefield, Uxbridge, Middlesex UB9 6NS 0870 050 0158
fax 08700 500 159; 190 stores mainly in southern England and East Anglia – for nearest store call 0800 526002
website www.budgens.co.uk hours Variable; usually Mon–Sat 8–8, Sun 10–4 cards Maestro, MasterCard, Solo, Visa.
✪ *These days you can be reasonably confident of going into Budgens and coming out with something you'd really like to drink.*

The Butlers Wine Cellar

247 Queens Park Road, Brighton BN2 9XJ (01273) 698724 fax (01273) 622761
e-mail henry@butlers-winecellar.co.uk website www.butlers-winecellar.co.uk
hours Tue–Sat 11–7, Sun 12–4 cards Access, Maestro, MasterCard, Visa delivery Free nationally over £150
en primeur Bordeaux. G M T
✪ *Henry Butler personally chooses the wines and there is some fascinating stuff there, including English wines from local growers such as Breaky Bottom and Ridgeview. Check the website or join the mailing list as offers change regularly.*

Anthony Byrne Fine Wines

mail order Ramsey Business Park, Stocking Fen Road, Ramsey, Cambs PE26 2UR (01487) 814555
fax (01487) 814962 e-mail anthony@abfw.co.uk or gary@abfw.co.uk website www.abfw.co.uk
hours Mon–Fri 9–5.30 cards MasterCard, Visa discounts Available on cases delivery Free 5 cases or more,
or orders of £250 or more; otherwise £12 minimum order 1 case en primeur Bordeaux, Burgundy, Rhône. C M T
✪ *A serious range of Burgundy; smaller but focused lists from Bordeaux and the Rhône; carefully selected wines from Alsace, Loire and Provence; and a wide range of New World.*

D Byrne & Co

Victoria Buildings, 12 King Street, Clitheroe, Lancashire BB7 2EP (01200) 423152
website www.dbyrne-finewines.co.uk
hours Mon–Sat 8.30–6 cards Maestro, MasterCard, Visa delivery Free within 50 miles; nationally £20 1st case,
£5 subsequent cases en primeur Bordeaux, Burgundy, Rhône, Germany. G M T
✪ *One of northern England's best wine merchants, with a hugely impressive range. I urge you to go see for yourself.*

Cambridge Wine Merchants

head office 29 Dry Drayton Industries, Scotland Road, Dry Drayton, CB23 8AT (01954) 214528
fax (01954) 214574 e-mail info@cambridgewine.com website www.cambridgewine.com
• 42 Mill Road, Cambridge CB1 2AD (01223) 568993 e-mail mill@cambridgewine.com
• 32 Bridge Street, Cambridge CB2 1UJ (01223) 568989 e-mail bridge@cambridgewine.com
• 2 King's Parade, Cambridge CB2 1SJ (01223) 309309 e-mail kings@cambridgewine.com
• 77 High Street, Huntingdon, PE29 3AN (01480) 414 745 e-mail huntingdon@cambridgewine.com
• 12 Church Street, Ampthill, MK45 2PL e-mail ampthill@cambridgewine.com
• 34b Kneesworth Street, Royston SG8 5AB (01763) 247076 e-mail royston@cambridgewine.com
• Edinburgh Wine Merchants, 30b Raeburn Place, Edinburgh (0131) 343 2347 e-mail stockbridge@edinburghwine.com
hours Mon–Sat 10am– 9pm, Sun 12–8 cards Amex, MasterCard, Switch, Visa discounts Buy 4, get the cheapest one
free (selected lines) delivery Free for 12 bottles or more within 5 miles of Cambridge; £2.50 for under 12 bottles. National
delivery £5.99 per case of 12 bottles; £9.99 for 1 to 11 bottles en primeur Bordeaux, Burgundy, Rhône, Port. C G M T
✪ *Young, unstuffy merchants with a well-chosen list: no dross, just a tight focus on good, individual producers, with
particularly interesting Australian, German, Champagne and dessert sections. They're also very serious about port –
as befits their university roots. Informative monthly newsletter. Every branch has a wine tasting club.*

Les Caves de Pyrene

Pew Corner, Old Portsmouth Road, Artington, Guildford GU3 1LP (office) (01483) 538820 (shop) (01483) 554750
fax (01483) 455068 e-mail sales@lescaves.co.uk website www.lescaves.co.uk
hours Mon–Fri 9–5 cards Maestro, MasterCard, Visa delivery Free for orders over £180 within M25, elsewhere at cost
discounts Negotiable minimum order 1 mixed case en primeur South-West France. G M T
✪ *Excellent operation, devoted to seeking out top wines from all over southern France. Other areas of France are looking
increasingly good too, Italy's regions are well represented, and there's some choice stuff from New Zealand.*

ChateauOnline

mail order 39 rue du Général Foy, 75008 Paris, France (00 33) 1 55 30 30 27
fax (00 33) 1 55 30 30 63 customer service 0800 169 2736 website www.chateauonline.com
hours Mon–Thurs 8–5, Fri 8–4 cards AmEx, Maestro, MasterCard, Visa, PayPal
delivery £14.99 per consignment, free for orders over £100 en primeur Bordeaux, Burgundy.
✪ *French specialist, with an impressive list of around 1500 wines. Easy-to-use website with a well-thought-out range of mixed cases, frequent special offers and bin end sales.*

Chilean Wine Club

online only 1 Cannon Meadow, Bull Lane, Gerrards Cross, Buckinghamshire SL9 8RE (01753) 890319
e-mail info@chileanwineclub.co.uk website www.chileanwineclub.co.uk
cards Delta, Maestro, MasterCard, Visa delivery £6.99 per address; free for orders over £250 in UK mainland; free to postcode SL9 irrespective of number of cases minimum order 1 mixed case.
✪ *A one-stop shop for many of Chile's finest wines that are not available on the high street.*

Cockburns of Leith

Cockburn House, Unit 3, Abbeyhill Industrial Estate, Abbey Lane, Edinburgh EH8 8HL (0131) 661 8400
fax (0131) 661 7333 e-mail sales@cockburnsofleith.co.uk website www.cockburnsofleith.co.uk
hours Mon–Fri 9–5; Sat 9–1 cards Maestro, MasterCard, Visa
delivery Free 12 or more bottles within Edinburgh; elsewhere £7 1–2 cases, free 3 cases or more
en primeur Bordeaux, Burgundy. G T
✪ *Clarets at bargain prices – in fact wines from all over France, including plenty of vins de pays. Among other countries New Zealand looks promising, and there's a great range of sherries.*

Colchester Wine Company

Gosbecks Park, Colchester, Essex CO2 9JJ (01206) 713560 fax (01206) 713515
e-mail sales@thewinecompany.co.uk website www.thewinecompany.co.uk
hours Mon–Sat 9–6 cards Delta, Electron, MasterCard, Maestro, Switch, Visa
delivery £7.99 or free for orders over £200 within UK mainland; please ring or email for quote for Highlands, islands and Northern Ireland. C G M T
✪ *Family-owned wine merchant, strong in French wines and wines from smaller estates, with plenty under £10. Well-chosen mixed case offers and regular tastings and dinners.*

Connolly's Wine Merchants

Arch 13, 220 Livery Street, Birmingham B3 1EU (0121) 236 9269/3837

fax (0121) 233 2339   website www.connollyswine.co.uk

hours Mon–Fri 9–5.30, Sat 10–4   cards AmEx, Maestro, MasterCard, Visa

delivery Surcharge outside Birmingham area   discounts 10% for cash & carry   en primeur Burgundy.   G M T

❂ *There's something for everyone here. Burgundy, Bordeaux and the Rhône all look very good; and there are top names from Germany, Italy, Spain and California. Monthly tutored tastings and winemaker dinners.*

The Co-operative Group (Co-op)

head office New Century House, Manchester M60 4ES Freephone 0800 068 6727 for stock details; approx. 3200 licensed stores, plus 800 Somerfield stores   e-mail customer.relations@co-op.co.uk   website www.co-operative.coop

hours Variable   cards Variable.

❂ *Champions of Fairtrade wines. Tasty stuff from around £5 and some real finds at £7–10. The Co-operative Group bought the Somerfield chain in March 2009 and is in the process of rebranding stores.*

Corney & Barrow

head office No. 1 Thomas More Street, London E1W 1YZ (020) 7265 2400   fax (020) 7265 2539

• Corney & Barrow East Anglia, Belvoir House, High Street, Newmarket CB8 8DH (01638) 600000

• Corney & Barrow (Scotland) with Whighams of Ayr, 8 Academy Street, Ayr KA7 1HT (01292) 267000 and Oxenfoord Castle, by Pathhead, Mid Lothian EH37 5UD (01875) 321921

e-mail wine@corneyandbarrow.com   website www.corneyandbarrow.com

hours Mon–Fri 8–6 (24-hr answering machine); Newmarket Mon–Sat 9–6; Edinburgh Mon–Fri 9–6; Ayr Mon–Fri 10–5.30, Sat 10–5.30   cards AmEx, Maestro, MasterCard, Visa   delivery Free for all orders above £200 within mainland UK, otherwise £12.50 per delivery. For Scotland and East Anglia, please contact the relevant office

en primeur Bordeaux, Burgundy, Champagne, Rhône, Italy, Spain.   C G M T

❂ *Top names in French and other European wines; Australia, South Africa and South America also impressive. Wines in every price bracket – try them out at Corney & Barrow wine bars in London.*

Croque-en-Bouche

mail order Old Post Office Cottage, Putley Green, Ledbury, Herefordshire HR8 2QN (01531) 670809

fax 08707 066282   e-mail mail@croque-en-bouche.co.uk   website www.croque-en-bouche.co.uk

hours By appointment 7 days a week   cards MasterCard, Visa, debit cards

discounts 3% for orders over £500 if paid by cheque or debit card delivery Free locally; elsewhere in England and Wales £5 per order; free in England and Wales for orders over £500 if paid by credit card; please ring or email for quote for Highlands, islands, Northern Ireland and elsewhere minimum order 1 mixed case (12 items) or £180. M
○ *A wonderful list, including older wines. Mature Australian reds from the 1990s; terrific stuff from the Rhône; some top clarets; and a generous sprinkling from other parts of the world.*

DeFINE Food & Wine
Chester Road, Sandiway, Cheshire CW8 2NH (01606) 882101
fax (01606) 888407 e-mail office@definefoodandwine.com website www.definefoodandwine.com
hours Mon–Thurs 10–7, Fri–Sat 10–8, Sun 12–6 cards AmEx, Maestro, MasterCard, Visa
discounts 5% off 12 bottles or more delivery Free locally, otherwise £10 UK minimum order 1 mixed case. C G M T
○ *Wine shop and delicatessen, with British cheeses and handmade pies and food specialities from Italy and Spain. Excellent, wide-ranging list of over 1000 wines including plenty of New World wines, as well as European classics.*

Devigne Wines
mail order PO Box 13748, North Berwick EH39 9AA (01620) 890860
fax (05600) 756 287 e-mail info@devignewines.co.uk website www.devignewines.co.uk
hours Mon–Fri 10–6 cards Maestro, MasterCard, Visa discounts Selected mixed cases at introductory rate
delivery Free for orders over £300, otherwise £6.50 per consignment; please ring for quote for Highlands and islands. M
○ *Small list specializing in French wine: traditional-method sparkling wines from all over France; a wide choice of rosés; Gaillac from the South-West; and wines from the Languedoc and the Jura.*

Direct Wine Shipments
5–7 Corporation Square, Belfast, Northern Ireland BT1 3AJ (028) 9050 8000
fax (028) 9050 8004 e-mail shop@directwine.co.uk and info@directwine.co.uk website www.directwine.co.uk
hours Mon–Fri 9.30–7 (Thur 10–8), Sat 9.30–5.30 cards Delta, Electron, Maestro, MasterCard, Solo, Switch, Visa
discounts 10% in the form of complementary wine with each case delivery Free Northern Ireland 1 case or more, variable delivery charge for UK mainland depending on customer spend en primeur Bordeaux, Burgundy, Rhône. C M T
○ *Rhône, Spain, Australia and Burgundy outstanding; Italy, Germany and Chile not far behind; there's good stuff from pretty much everywhere. Wine courses, tastings and expert advice offered.*

The following services are available where indicated: C = cellarage **G** = glass hire/loan **M** = mail/online order **T** = tastings and talks

Nick Dobson Wines

mail order 38 Crail Close, Wokingham, Berkshire RG41 2PZ 0800 849 3078
fax 0870 460 2358 e-mail nick.dobson@nickdobsonwines.co.uk website www.nickdobsonwines.co.uk
hours Mon–Sat 9–5 cards Access, Maestro, MasterCard, Visa
delivery £8.95 + VAT 1 case; £6.60 + VAT 2nd and subsequent cases to UK mainland addresses. Free local delivery. M T
✪ *Specialist in wines from Switzerland, Austria and Beaujolais, plus intriguing selections from elsewhere in Europe.*

Domaine Direct

mail order 6–9 Cynthia Street, London N1 9JF (020) 7837 1142
fax (020) 7837 8605 e-mail mail@domainedirect.co.uk website www.domainedirect.co.uk
hours 8.30–6 or answering machine cards Maestro, MasterCard, Visa
delivery Free London; elsewhere in UK mainland 1 case £15, 2 cases £21, 3 cases £23.50, 4 or more free
and for all orders over £400 + VAT minimum order 1 mixed case en primeur Burgundy. C M T
✪ *Sensational Burgundy list; prices are very reasonable for the quality. Also the Burgundian-style Chardonnays
from Australia's Leeuwin Estate.*

Farr Vintners

220 Queenstown Road, Battersea, London SW8 4LP (020) 7821 2000
fax (020) 7821 2020 e-mail sales@farrvintners.com website www.farrvintners.com
hours Mon–Fri 9–6 cards Access, Maestro, MasterCard, Visa delivery London £1 per case (min £15); elsewhere
at cost minimum order £500 + VAT en primeur Bordeaux. C M T
✪ *A fantastic list of the world's finest wines. The majority is Bordeaux, but you'll also find top stuff and older vintages
of white Burgundy, red Rhône, plus Italy, Australia and California.*

Fingal-Rock

64 Monnow Street, Monmouth NP25 3EN
tel & fax 01600 712372 e-mail tom@pinotnoir.co.uk website www.pinotnoir.co.uk
hours Mon 9.30–1.30, Thurs & Fri 9.30–5.30, Sat 9.30–5 cards Maestro, MasterCard, Visa discounts 5% for
at least 12 bottles collected from shop, 7.5% for collected orders over £500, 10% for collected orders over £1200
delivery Free locally (within 30 miles); orders further afield free if over £100. G M T
✪ *The list's great strength is Burgundy, from some very good growers and priced between £8 and £40.
Small but tempting selections from other French regions, as well as other parts of Europe and the New World.*

Flagship Wines

417 Hatfield Road, St Albans, Hertfordshire AL4 0XP (01727) 865309
e-mail sales@flagshipwines.co.uk website www.flagshipwines.co.uk
hours Tues–Thurs 11–6, Fri 11–7.30, Sat 10–6 cards Maestro, MasterCard, Visa
delivery Free to St Albans addresses and £10 to other UK mainland addresses. G M T
✪ *Independent whose prices can match those of the supermarkets – with the friendly, well-informed advice of boss Julia Jenkins thrown in. Strong in Australia, New Zealand and France but great stuff all round. Programme of tastings and events.*

The Flying Corkscrew

Leighton Buzzard Road, Water End, Nr Hemel Hempstead, Hertfordshire HP1 3BD (01442) 412311
fax (01442) 412313 e-mail sales@flyingcorkscrew.co.uk website www.flyingcorkscrew.co.uk
hours Mon–Thurs 10–7, Fri 10–8, Sat 10–6, Sun 11–4 cards AmEx, Maestro, MasterCard, Visa
discounts 5% on 6 bottles, 15% on 12 bottles (mixed) delivery Free for orders over £150; £15 per case under £150.
G M T
✪ *Extensive and imaginative range of wines from every corner of France. Italy, Australia and the US are terrific. Friendly, knowledgeable staff – and if you're local, look out for tastings led by experts and winemakers.*

Fortnum & Mason

181 Piccadilly, London W1A 1ER (020) 7734 8040
fax (020) 7437 3278 ordering line (020) 7973 4136 e-mail info@fortnumandmason.co.uk
website www.fortnumandmason.com hours Mon–Sat 10–8, Sun 12–6 (Food Hall and Patio Restaurant only)
cards AmEx, Diners, Maestro, MasterCard, Visa discounts 1 free bottle per unmixed dozen
delivery £7 per delivery address en primeur Bordeaux. M T
✪ *Impressive names from just about everywhere, including Champagne, Bordeaux, Burgundy, Italy, Germany, Australia, New Zealand, South Africa and California. Impeccably sourced own-label range.*

Friarwood

26 New King's Road, London SW6 4ST (020) 7736 2628 fax (020) 7731 0411
e-mail simon.mckay@friarwood.com; christina@friarwood.com
• 16 Dock Street, Leith, Edinburgh EH6 6EY (0131) 554 4159 fax (0131) 554 6703 e-mail edinburgh@friarwood.com
website www.friarwood.com hours Mon–Sat 10–7
cards AmEx, Diners, Maestro, MasterCard, Visa, Solo, Electron discounts 5% on cases on 12 (mixed and unmixed)

delivery (London) Free within M25 and on orders over £200 in mainland UK; (Edinburgh) free locally and on orders over £200 en primeur Bordeaux. C G M T

✪ *The focus is Bordeaux, including mature wines from a good selection of petits châteaux as well as classed growths. Burgundy and other French regions are strong too.*

FromVineyardsDirect.com

online only Northburgh House, 10 Northburgh Street, London EC1V 0AT (020) 7490 9910
fax (020) 7490 3708 e-mail info@fromvineyardsdirect.com website www.fromvineyardsdirect.com
hours 9–7 cards Maestro, MasterCard, Visa, Solo, Switch
delivery Free minimum order 1 case (12 bottles) in UK mainland; 2 cases in Northern Ireland, Scottish Highlands and islands en primeur Bordeaux. C M T

✪ *A hand-picked selection of wines direct from vineyards in France, Italy and Spain, at very affordable prices.*

Gauntleys of Nottingham

4 High Street, Exchange Arcade, Nottingham NG1 2ET (0115) 911 0555
fax (0115) 911 0557 e-mail rhône@gauntleywine.com website www.gauntleywine.com
hours Mon–Sat 9–5.30 cards Maestro, MasterCard, Visa
delivery 1 case £11.95, 2–3 cases £9.50, 4 or more cases free minimum order 1 case
en primeur Alsace, Burgundy, Loire, Rhône, southern France, Spain. M T

✪ *They've won awards for their Rhône and Alsace lists. The Loire, Burgundy, southern France and Spain are also excellent.*

Goedhuis & Co

6 Rudolf Place, Miles Street, London SW8 1RP (020) 7793 7900
fax (020) 7793 7170 e-mail sales@goedhuis.com website www.goedhuis.com
hours Mon–Fri 9–5.30 cards Maestro, MasterCard, Visa
delivery Free on orders over £250 ex-VAT; otherwise £15 England, elsewhere at cost minimum order 1 unmixed case
en primeur Bordeaux, Burgundy, Rhône. C G M T

✪ *Fine wine specialist. Bordeaux, Burgundy and the Rhône are the core of the list, but everything is good.*

Great Northern Wine

The Warehouse, Blossomgate, Ripon, North Yorkshire HG4 2AJ (01765) 606767
fax (01765) 609151 e-mail info@greatnorthernwine.co.uk website www.greatnorthernwine.co.uk

hours Tues–Wed 9–7, Thurs–Sat 9–11 cards AmEx, Maestro, MasterCard, Visa discounts 10% on case quantities
delivery Free locally, elsewhere at cost en primeur Bordeaux. G M T
✪ *Independent shippers who seek out interesting wines from around the world. There's also a wine bar, where you can enjoy wines bought in the shop (£5 corkage charge).*

Great Western Wine

Wells Road, Bath BA2 3AP (01225) 322810 (enquiries) or (01225) 322820 (orders)
fax (01225) 442139 e-mail wine@greatwesternwine.co.uk website www.greatwesternwine.co.uk
hours Mon–Fri 10–7, Sat 10–6 cards AmEx, Maestro, MasterCard, Visa
discounts 5% off mixed cases, 8% off unsplit cases delivery Free for 12 bottles or more in UK mainland; £8.95
for smaller orders en primeur Australia, Bordeaux, Burgundy, Rioja. C G M T
✪ *Wide-ranging list, bringing in brilliant wines from individual growers around the world. Also organizes events and tastings.*

Peter Green & Co

37A/B Warrender Park Road, Edinburgh EH9 1HJ (0131) 229 5925
e-mail shop@petergreenwines.com hours Tues–Thur 10–6.30, Fri 10–7.30, Sat 10–6.30
cards Maestro, MasterCard, Visa discounts 5% on unmixed half-dozens delivery Free in Edinburgh
minimum order (For delivery) 1 case. G T
✪ *Extensive and adventurous list: Tunisia, India and the Lebanon rub shoulders with France, Italy and Germany.*

Green & Blue

36–38 Lordship Lane, East Dulwich, London, SE22 8HJ (020) 8693 9250
e-mail info@greenandbluewines.com website www.greenandbluewines.com
hours Mon–Wed 9–11, Thur–Sat 9–midnight, Sun 11–10
cards Delta, Maestro, MasterCard, Visa discounts 5% off mixed cases of 12 (collection only), 10% on unmixed cases
delivery Free within 2 miles for over £200, otherwise £10 per delivery within M25; £10 per case outside M25. G T
✪ *A tempting list full of unusual, intriguing wines you really want to drink – and you can try them on the spot, in the wine bar, which serves tapas-style food. The staff are knowledgeable, and there's a waiting list for the popular tutored tastings.*

Haddows See Wine Rack.

The following services are available where indicated: **C** = cellarage **G** = glass hire/loan **M** = mail/online order **T** = tastings and talks

Halifax Wine Company

18 Prescott Street, Halifax, West Yorkshire HX1 2LG (01422) 256333
e-mail andy@halifaxwinecompany.com website www.halifaxwinecompany.com hours Tues–Wed 9–5, Thur–Fri 9–6,
Sat 9–5. Closed first week in January and first week in August cards Access, Maestro, MasterCard, Visa
discounts 8% on 12 bottles or more for personal callers to the shop delivery Free in West Yorkshire on orders over £85;
rest of UK mainland £5.95 for first 12 bottles then £4.95 per subsequent case. M
✪ *Exciting, wide-ranging and award-winning list, at keen prices.*

Handford Wines

105 Old Brompton Road, South Kensington, London SW7 3LE (020) 7589 6113 fax (020) 7581 2983
e-mail jack@handford.net website www.handford.net hours Mon–Sat 10–8.30, Sun 12–4
cards AmEx, MasterCard, Visa discounts 5% on mixed cases delivery £8.50 for orders under £150 within UK
en primeur Bordeaux, Burgundy, Rhône, Port. G M T
✪ *Delightful London shop, absolutely packed with the sort of wines I really want to drink.*

Roger Harris Wines

mail order Loke Farm, Weston Longville, Norfolk NR9 5LG (01603) 880171
fax (01603) 880291 e-mail sales@rogerharriswines.co.uk website www.rogerharriswines.co.uk
hours Mon–Fri 9–5 cards AmEx, MasterCard, Visa
delivery UK mainland, £3 for orders up to £110, £2 up to £160, free over £160 minimum order 1 mixed case. M
✪ *Britain's acknowledged experts in Beaujolais also have a good range of whites from the neighbouring Mâconnais region.*

Harvey Nichols

109–125 Knightsbridge, London SW1X 7RJ (020) 7235 5000
• The Mailbox, 31–32 Wharfside Street, Birmingham B1 1RE (0121) 616 6000
• 30–34 St Andrew Square, Edinburgh EH2 2AD (0131) 524 8388
• 107–111 Briggate, Leeds LS1 6AZ (0113) 204 8888
• 21 New Cathedral Street, Manchester M1 1AD (0161) 828 8888
website www.harveynichols.com
hours (London) Mon–Fri 10–8, Sat 10–7, Sun 12–6; (Birmingham) Mon–Wed 10–6, Thurs 10–8, Fri–Sat 10–7, Sun 11–5;
(Edinburgh) Mon–Wed 10–6, Thurs 10–8, Fri, Sat 10–7, Sun 11–6; (Leeds) Mon–Wed 10–6, Thurs 10–8, Fri–Sat 10–7,
Sun 11–5; (Manchester) Mon, Wed, Fri 10–7, Thurs 10–8, Sat 10–6, Sun 11–5

cards AmEx, Maestro, MasterCard, Visa.

○ *Sought-after producers and cult fine wines, especially from France, Italy and California.*

Haynes Hanson & Clark

Sheep Street, Stow-on-the-Wold, Gloucestershire GL54 1AA (01451) 870808   fax (01451) 870508

• 7 Elystan Street, London SW3 3NT (020) 7584 7927   fax (020) 7584 7967

e-mail stow@hhandc.co.uk or london@hhandc.co.uk   website www.hhandc.co.uk

hours (Stow) Mon–Fri 9–6, Sat 9–5.30; (London) Mon–Fri 9–7, Sat 9–4.30   cards Access, Maestro, MasterCard, Visa

discounts 10% unsplit case   delivery Free for 1 case or more in central London and areas covered by Stow-on-the-Wold

van; elsewhere 1 case £14.95, 2–3 cases £9.35 per case, 4 or more cases £7.70 per case, free on orders over £650

en primeur Bordeaux, Burgundy.   M T

○ *Known for its subtle, elegant wines: top-notch Burgundy is the main focus of the list, but other French regions*
are well represented, and there's interesting stuff from Spain, Italy, Australia and New Zealand.

Hedley Wright

11 Twyford Centre, London Road, Bishop's Stortford, Herts CM23 3YT (01279) 465818   fax (01279) 465819

• Wyevale Garden Centre, Cambridge Road, Hitchin, Herts, SG4 0JT (01462) 431110   fax (01462) 422983

e-mail sales@hedleywright.co.uk   website www.hedleywright.co.uk   hours Mon–Wed 9–6, Thur–Fri 9–7, Sat 10–6;

(Hitchin) Mon–Wed 11–7, Thur–Fri 11–8, Sat 11–7, Sun 11–5   cards AmEx, Maestro, MasterCard, Visa   delivery £5 per

delivery, free for orders over £100   minimum order 1 mixed case   en primeur Bordeaux, Chile, Germany, Port.   C G M T

○ *A good all-round list, especially strong in France, Italy, Spain and South Africa.*

Hicks & Don

4 Old Station Yard, Edington, Westbury, Wiltshire BA13 4NT (01380) 831234   fax (01380) 831010

e-mail mailbox@hicksanddon.co.uk   website www.hicksanddon.co.uk   hours Mon–Fri 9–5

cards Maestro, MasterCard, Visa   discounts Negotiable   delivery Free over £100, otherwise £6 per case in UK mainland

minimum order 1 case   en primeur Bordeaux, Burgundy, Chile, Italy, Port, Rhône.   C G M T

○ *Subtle, well-made wines that go with food, particularly French wines. Still plenty under £10.*

Jeroboams (incorporating Laytons)

head office 7–9 Elliot's Place, London N1 8HX (020) 7288 8888   fax (020) 7359 2616

shops 50–52 Elizabeth Street, London SW1W 9PB (020) 7730 8108

- 20 Davies Street, London W1K 3DT (020) 7499 1015 • 13 Elgin Crescent, London W11 2JA (020) 7229 0527
- 29 Heath Street, London NW3 6TR (020) 7435 6845 • 96 Holland Park Avenue, London W11 3RB (020) 7727 9359
- 6 Pont Street, London SW1X 9EL (020) 7235 1612 • 1 St John's Wood High Street, London NW8 7NG (020) 7722 4020
- 56 Walton Street, London SW3 1RB (020) 7589 2020
- Mr Christian's Delicatessen, 11 Elgin Crescent, London W11 2JA (020) 7229 0501
- Milroy's of Soho, 3 Greek Street, London W1D 4NX (020) 7437 2385 (whisky and wine)

e-mail sales@jeroboams.co.uk website www.jeroboams.co.uk hours Offices Mon–Fri 9–5.30, shops Mon–Sat 9–7 (may vary) cards AmEx, Maestro, MasterCard, Visa delivery Free for orders over £200, otherwise £9.95
en primeur Bordeaux, Burgundy, Rhône. C G M T
✪ *Wide-ranging list of affordable and enjoyable wines, especially good in France, Italy, Australia and New Zealand. Fine foods, especially cheeses and olive oils, are available in the Holland Park and Mr Christian's Delicatessen shops.*

S H Jones

27 High Street, Banbury, Oxfordshire OX16 5EW (01295) 251179 fax (01295) 272352 e-mail banbury@shjones.com
- 9 Market Square, Bicester, Oxfordshire OX26 6AA (01869) 322448 e-mail bicester@shjones.com
- The Cellar Shop, 2 Riverside, Tramway Road, Banbury, Oxfordshire OX16 5TU (01295) 672296 fax (01295) 259560
e-mail retail@shjones.com
- 121 Regent Street, Leamington Spa, Warwickshire CV32 4NU (01926) 315609 e-mail leamington@shjones.com
website www.shjones.com hours Please call each store for details cards Maestro, MasterCard, Visa
delivery Free for 12 bottles of wine/spirits or total value over £100 within 15-mile radius of shops, otherwise £9.75
per case en primeur Bordeaux, Burgundy, Port. C G M T
✪ *Wide-ranging list with good Burgundies and Rhônes, clarets from under a tenner to top names and plenty of tasty stuff from elsewhere – southern France to South America. There is a wine bar at the High Street shop in Banbury.*

Justerini & Brooks

mail order 61 St James's Street, London SW1A 1LZ (020) 7484 6400 fax (020) 7484 6499
e-mail justorders@justerinis.com website www.justerinis.com
hours Mon–Fri 9–5.30 cards Maestro, MasterCard, Visa
delivery Free for unmixed cases over £250, otherwise £15 UK mainland minimum order 1 case
en primeur Alsace, Bordeaux, Burgundy, Italy, Loire, Rhône, Germany. C M T
✪ *Superb list of top-quality wines from Europe's classic regions, as well as some excellent New World choices. While some wines are very pricey, there is plenty for around a tenner.*

Laithwaites Wine

mail order New Aquitaine House, Exeter Way, Theale, Reading, Berkshire RG7 4PL order line 0845 194 7700
fax 0845 194 7766 e-mail orders@laithwaites.co.uk website www.laithwaites.co.uk
hours Mon–Fri 8–11, Sat–Sun 8–9 cards AmEx, Diners, Maestro, MasterCard, Visa
discounts On unmixed cases of 6 or 12 delivery £6.99 per delivery address
en primeur Australia, Bordeaux, Burgundy, Rhône, Rioja. C M T
✪ *Extensive selection of wines from France, Australia, Spain, Italy and elsewhere. Informative website has excellent mixed cases, while the bin ends and special offers are good value.*

Lay & Wheeler

mail order Holton Park, Holton St Mary, Suffolk CO7 6NN 0845 330 1855 fax 0845 330 4095
e-mail sales@laywheeler.com website www.laywheeler.com
hours (Order office) Mon–Fri 8.30–5.30 cards Maestro, MasterCard, Visa delivery £9.95; free for orders over £200
en primeur Bordeaux, Burgundy, Port (some vintages), Rhône, Spain. C M T
✪ *First-class Bordeaux and Burgundy to satisfy the most demanding drinker, and plenty more besides. A must-have list.*

Laymont & Shaw

The Old Chapel, Millpool, Truro, Cornwall TR1 1EX (01872) 270545
e-mail sales@laymont-shaw.co.uk website www.laymont-shaw.co.uk
hours Mon–Wed 10–5.30, Thur–Sat 10–6.30 cards Maestro, MasterCard, Visa
delivery £8.50 per case UK mainland; free for orders over £200 minimum order 1 mixed case. G M T
✪ *Excellent, knowledgeable list that specializes in Spain and Portugal, plus wines from Italy, France and elsewhere.*

Lea & Sandeman

170 Fulham Road, London SW10 9PR (020) 7244 0522 fax (020) 7244 0533
● 51 High Street, Barnes, London SW13 9LN (020) 8878 8643 ● 211 Kensington Church Street, London W8 7LX (020) 7221 1982 ● 167 Chiswick High Road, London W4 2DR (020) 7244 0522 e-mail info@leaandsandeman.co.uk
website www.londonfinewine.co.uk hours Mon–Sat 10–8 cards AmEx, Maestro, MasterCard, Visa
discounts 5–15% by case, other discounts on 10 cases or more delivery London £10 for less than £100, otherwise free, and to UK mainland south of Perth on orders over £250 en primeur Bordeaux, Burgundy, Italy. C G M T
✪ *Burgundy and Italy take precedence here, and there's a succession of excellent names, chosen with great care. Bordeaux has wines at all price levels, and there are short but fascinating ranges from the USA, Spain, Australia and New Zealand.*

Liberty Wines

mail order Unit D18, The Food Market, New Covent Garden, London SW8 5LL (020) 7720 5350
fax (020) 7720 6158 website www.libertywine.co.uk e-mail order@libertywine.co.uk hours Mon–Fri 9–5.30
cards Maestro, MasterCard, Visa delivery Free to mainland UK minimum order 12 x 75cl bottles. M
✪ *Italy rules, with superb wines from pretty well all the best producers. Liberty are the UK agents for most of their producers, so if you're interested in Italian wines, this should be your first port of call. Also top names from Australia and elsewhere.*

Linlithgow Wines

Crossford, Station Road, Linlithgow, West Lothian EH49 6BW tel & fax (01506) 848821
e-mail jrobmcd@aol.com website www.linlithgowwines.co.uk hours Mon–Fri 9–5.30 (please phone first)
cards None: cash, cheque or bank transfer only delivery Free locally; elsewhere in UK £9 for 1 case, £7 per case for 2 or more. G M T
✪ *Terrific list of French wines, many imported direct from family-run vineyards in southern France, and many around £5–7.*

The Local See Wine Rack.

O W Loeb & Co

mail order 3 Archie Street, off Tanner Street, London SE1 3JT (020) 7234 0385
fax (020) 7357 0440 e-mail finewine@owloeb.com website www.owloeb.com hours Mon–Fri 8.30–5.30
cards Maestro, MasterCard, Visa discounts 3 cases and above delivery Free 3 cases or more and on orders over £250
minimum order 1 case en primeur Burgundy, Bordeaux, Rhône, Germany (Mosel). C M T
✪ *Burgundy, the Rhône, Loire and Germany stand out, with top producers galore. Then there are Loeb's new discoveries from Spain and the New World, especially New Zealand and South Africa.*

Maison du Vin

Moor Hill, Hawkhurst, Kent TN18 4PF (01580) 753487
fax (01580) 755627 e-mail kvgriffin@aol.com website www.maison-du-vin.co.uk
hours Mon 10–4, Tue–Fri 10–5, Sat 10–6 cards Access, AmEx, Maestro, MasterCard, Visa
delivery Free locally; UK mainland at cost en primeur Bordeaux. C G M T
✪ *As the name suggests, the focus is on French wines – with some good stuff from Australia and Chile – at prices from about £6 upwards. There's a monthly themed 'wine school' or you can book personal tutored tastings.*

Majestic

(see also Wine and Beer World page 188)

head office Majestic House, Otterspool Way, Watford, Herts WD25 8WW (01923) 298200
fax (01923) 819105; 150 stores nationwide e-mail info@majestic.co.uk website www.majestic.co.uk
hours Mon–Fri 10–8, Sat 9–7, Sun 10–5 (may vary) cards AmEx, Diners, Maestro, MasterCard, Visa
delivery Free UK mainland minimum order 1 mixed case (12 bottles) en primeur Bordeaux, Port, Burgundy. G M T
○ *One of the best places to buy Champagne, with a good range and good discounts for buying in quantity.*
Loads of interesting and reasonably priced stuff, especially from France, Germany and the New World.

Marks & Spencer

head office Waterside House, 35 North Wharf Road, London W2 1NW (020) 7935 4422
fax (020) 7487 2679; 600 licensed stores website www.marksandspencer.com hours Variable
discounts Variable, a selection of 10 different Wines of the Month, buy any 6 and save 10% in selected stores. M T
○ *M&S works with top producers around the world to create its impressive list of own-label wines.*
All the wines are exclusive and unique to M&S, selected and blended by their in-house winemaking team.

Martinez Wines

35 The Grove, Ilkley, Leeds, West Yorkshire LS29 9NJ (01943) 600000
fax 0870 922 3940 e-mail shop@martinez.co.uk website www.martinez.co.uk
hours Sun 12–6, Mon–Wed 10–8, Thurs–Fri 10–9, Sat 9.30–6 cards AmEx, Maestro, MasterCard, Visa
discounts 5% on 6 bottles or more, 10% on orders over £150 delivery Free local delivery, otherwise £13.99
per case mainland UK en primeur Bordeaux, Burgundy. C G M T
○ *From a wide-ranging list, I'd single out the selections from France, Italy, Spain, Australia, Argentina and South Africa.*

Millésima

mail order 87 Quai de Paludate, BP 89, 33038 Bordeaux Cedex, France (00 33) 5 57 80 88 08
fax (00 33) 5 57 80 88 19 Freephone 0800 917 0352 website www.millesima.com hours Mon–Fri 8–5.30
cards AmEx, Diners, Maestro, MasterCard, Visa delivery For bottled wines, free to single UK addresses for orders
exceeding £500. Otherwise, a charge of £20 will be applied. For en primeur wines, free to single UK addresses.
en primeur Bordeaux, Burgundy, Rhône. M T
○ *Wine comes direct from the châteaux to Millésima's cellars, where 3 million bottles are stored.*
A sprinkling of established names from other French regions.

Montrachet

mail order 11 Catherine Place, London SW1E 6DX (020) 7928 1990

fax (020) 7928 3415 e-mail charles@montrachetwine.com website www.montrachetwine.com

hours Mon–Fri 8.30–5.30 cards Maestro, MasterCard, Visa delivery England and Wales £15, free for 3 or more cases;
for Scotland ring for details minimum order 1 unmixed case

en primeur Bordeaux, Burgundy. M T

✪ *Impressive Burgundies are the main attraction here, but there are also some very good Rhônes,
and Bordeaux is excellent at all price levels.*

Moreno Wines

11 Marylands Road, London W9 2DU (020) 7286 0678

fax (020) 7286 0513 e-mail merchant@moreno-wines.co.uk website www.morenowinedirect.com

hours Mon–Fri 4–8, Sat 12–8 cards AmEx, Maestro, MasterCard, Visa discounts 10% on 1 or more cases

delivery Up to 1 case £8, up to 2 cases £10, free thereafter. M T

✪ *Specialist in Spanish wines, from everyday drinking to fine and rare wines from older vintages, with a few well-chosen
additions from Australia, Italy and elsewhere.*

Wm Morrisons Supermarkets

head office Hilmore House, Gain Lane, Bradford, West Yorkshire BD3 7DL 0845 611 5000

fax 0845 611 6801 customer service 0845 611 6111; 371 licensed branches website www.morrisons.co.uk

hours Variable, generally Mon–Sat 8–8, Sun 10–4 cards AmEx, Delta, Maestro, MasterCard, Solo, Style, Visa Electron. G T

✪ *Inexpensive, often tasty wines, and if you're prepared to trade up a little there's some really good stuff here.*

New Zealand House of Wine

mail order/online based near Petworth, Surrey

e-mail info@nzhouseofwine.com website www.nzhouseofwine.com

order freephone 0800 085 6273 enquiries (01428) 70 77 33 fax (01428) 70 77 66

hours Mon–Fri, UK office hours cards AmEx, Delta, Maestro, MasterCard, Visa

discounts 10% on high-volume orders (60+ bottles) for parties, weddings etc

delivery £5.99 UK mainland (£9.59 for less than 12 bottles); see website Delivery Details for other regions. M

✪ *Impressive list of over 300 New Zealand wines, with plenty under £10 and some really fine stuff around £20 and over.*

James Nicholson

7/9 Killyleagh Street, Crossgar, Co. Down, Northern Ireland BT30 9DQ (028) 4483 0091
fax (028) 4483 0028 e-mail shop@jnwine.com website www.jnwine.com hours Mon–Sat 10–7
cards Maestro, MasterCard, Visa discounts 10% mixed case delivery Free (1 case or more) in Eire and Northern
Ireland; UK mainland £10.95, 2 cases £15.95 en primeur Bordeaux, Burgundy, California, Rioja, Rhône. C G M T
✪ *Well-chosen list mainly from small, committed growers around the world. Bordeaux, Rhône and southern France are
slightly ahead of the field, there's a good selection of Burgundy and some excellent drinking from Germany and Spain.*

Nickolls & Perks

37 Lower High Street, Stourbridge, West Midlands DY8 1TA (01384) 394518
fax (01384) 440786 e-mail sales@nickollsandperks.co.uk website www.nickollsandperks.co.uk
hours Tues–Fri 10.30–5.30, Sat 10.30–5 cards Maestro, MasterCard, Visa discounts negotiable per case
delivery £10 per consignment; free over £150 en primeur Bordeaux, Champagne, Port. C G M T
✪ *Established in 1797, Nickolls & Perks have a wide-ranging list – and a terrific website – covering most areas.
Their strength is France. Advice is available to clients wishing to develop their cellars or invest in wine.*

Nidderdale Fine Wines

2a High Street, Pateley Bridge, North Yorkshire HG3 5AW (01423) 711703
e-mail info@southaustralianwines.com website www.southaustralianwines.com hours Tues–Sat 10–6
cards Maestro, MasterCard, Visa discounts 5% case discount on shop purchases for 12+ bottles
delivery £5 per 12-bottle case in England, Wales and southern Scotland. Single bottle delivery available. G T
✪ *Specialist in South Australia, with 300 wines broken down into regions. Also 350 or so wines from the rest of the world.
Look out for online offers and winemaker dinners.*

Noble Rot Wine Warehouses

18 Market Street, Bromsgrove, Worcestershire, B61 8DA (01527) 575606 fax (01527) 833133
e-mail info@noble-rot.co.uk website www.noble-rot.co.uk hours Tues–Fri 10–6, Sat & Mon 9.30–5.30
cards Maestro, MasterCard, Visa discounts Various delivery Free within 10-mile radius. G T
✪ *Australia, Italy, France and Spain feature strongly in a frequently changing list of more than 400 wines,
mostly at £5–15.*

The following services are available where indicated: **C** = cellarage **G** = glass hire/loan **M** = mail/online order **T** = tastings and talks

O'Briens

head office 33 Spruce Avenue, Stillorgan Industrial Park, Co. Dublin, Ireland (low cost number) 1850 269 777
fax 01 269 7480; 27 stores e-mail sales@obrienswines.ie; info@obrienswines.ie website www.wine.ie
hours Mon–Sat 10am–11pm, Sun 1–11pm cards MasterCard, Visa delivery €10 per case anywhere in Ireland (minimum order 6 bottles); free for orders over €200 en primeur Bordeaux. G M T
✪ *Family-owned drinks retailer, which could well claim to be the best of the chains in Ireland. Imports directly from over 75 wineries worldwide.*

Oddbins

head office 31–33 Weir Road, London SW19 8UG (020) 8944 4400; 131 shops nationwide fax (020) 8944 4411
mail order Oddbins Direct 0800 328 2323 fax 0800 328 3848 website www.oddbins.com
hours Vary cards AmEx, Maestro, MasterCard, Visa discounts 20% off any 12 bottles of wine or more
delivery Free locally for orders over £100 en primeur Bordeaux. G M T
• Oddbins Calais Parc la Française, Avenue Charles de Gaulle, Coquelles, Calais, France (00 33) 3 2119 0019
fax (00 33) 3 2100 0010 website www.oddbins-calais.com pre-order online Free return ferry crossing when you pre-order £250 or more hours 7 days, 9–9.
✪ *New World meets the classic regions of Europe: extensive Aussie selection, well-chosen Chilean, Argentine and South African wines sit alongside good stuff from France, Spain and Italy. Always a great range of fizz.*

The Oxford Wine Company

The Wine Warehouse, Witney Road, Standlake, Oxon OX29 7PR (01865) 301144
fax (01865) 301155 e-mail orders@oxfordwine.co.uk website www.oxfordwine.co.uk
hours Mon–Sat 9–7, Sun 11–4 cards AmEx, Diners, Maestro, MasterCard, Visa discounts 5% discount on a case of 12, no minimum order delivery Free locally; national delivery £9.99 for any amount en primeur Bordeaux. G M T
✪ *A good selection from the classic regions and the New World, from bargain basement prices to expensive fine wines. Easy-to-use website. They also organize tastings and other events.*

OZ WINES

mail order Freepost Lon 17656, London SW18 5BR, 0845 450 1261
fax (020) 8870 8839 e-mail sales@ozwines.co.uk website www.ozwines.co.uk hours Mon–Fri 9.30–7
cards Access, Diners, Maestro, MasterCard, Visa delivery Free minimum order 1 mixed case. M T
✪ *Australian wines made by small wineries and real people – with the thrilling flavours that Australians do better than anyone.*

Penistone Court Wine Cellars

The Railway Station, Penistone, Sheffield, South Yorkshire S36 6HP (01226) 766037
fax (01226) 767310 e-mail chris@pcwine.plus.com website www.pcwine.co.uk
hours Tues–Fri 10–6, Sat 10–3 cards Maestro, MasterCard, Visa
delivery Free locally, rest of UK mainland charged at cost 1 case or more minimum order 1 case. G M
✪ *A well-balanced list, with something from just about everywhere, mostly from familiar names.*

Philglas & Swiggot

21 Northcote Road, Battersea, London SW11 1NG (020) 7924 4494
• 64 Hill Rise, Richmond, London TW10 6UB (020) 8332 6031
• 22 New Quebec Street, Marylebone, London W1H 7SB (020) 7402 0002
e-mail info@philglas-swiggot.co.uk website www.philglas-swiggot.co.uk
hours Mon–Sat 11–7, Sun 12–5 cards AmEx, Maestro, MasterCard, Visa
discounts 5% per case delivery Free 1 case locally. G M
✪ *Excellent selections from Australia, Italy, France and Austria – subtle, interesting wines, not blockbuster brands.*

Christopher Piper Wines

1 Silver Street, Ottery St Mary, Devon EX11 1DB (01404) 814139
fax (01404) 812100 e-mail sales@christopherpiperwines.co.uk website www.christopherpiperwines.co.uk
hours Mon–Fri 8.30–5.30, Sat 9–4.30 cards Maestro, MasterCard, Visa
discounts 5% mixed case, 10% 3 or more cases delivery £8.95 for 1 case then £4.80 for each case,
free for orders over £220 minimum order (for mail order) 1 mixed case
en primeur Bordeaux, Burgundy, Rhône. C G M T
✪ *Huge range of well-chosen wines that reflect a sense of place and personality, with lots of information to help you make up your mind.*

Terry Platt Wine Merchants

Council Street West, Llandudno LL30 1ED (01492) 874099
fax (01492) 874788 e-mail info@terryplattwines.co.uk website www.terryplattwines.co.uk
hours Mon–Fri 8.30–5.30 cards Access, Maestro, MasterCard, Visa
delivery Free locally and UK mainland 5 cases or more minimum order 1 mixed case. G M T
✪ *A wide-ranging list with a sprinkling of good growers from most regions. New World coverage has increased recently.*

Playford Ros

Middle Park, Thirsk, Yorkshire YO7 3AH (01845) 526777
fax (01845) 526888 e-mail sales@playfordros.com website www.playfordros.com
hours Mon–Fri 8–5 cards MasterCard, Visa
discounts Negotiable delivery Free Yorkshire, Derbyshire, Durham, Newcastle; elsewhere £10–15 or at courier
cost minimum order 1 mixed case en primeur Bordeaux, Burgundy. G M T
✪ *A carefully chosen list, with reassuringly recognizable Burgundy, exceptional Australian and good stuff from other French regions, Chile, Oregon and New Zealand. Plenty at the £6–8 mark.*

Portland Wine Co

152a Ashley Road, Hale WA15 9SA (0161) 928 0357
fax (0161) 905 1291 e-mail info@portlandwine.co.uk website www.portlandwine.co.uk
hours Mon–Fri 10–9, Sat 9–9 cards Maestro, MasterCard, Visa discounts 5% on 2 cases or more, 10% on 5 cases
or more delivery Free locally, £15 + VAT per consignment nationwide, no minimum order en primeur Bordeaux. C T
✪ *Spain, Portugal and Burgundy are specialities and there's a promising-looking list of clarets. Consumer-friendly list with something at every price level from around the world.*

Private Cellar

mail order 51 High Street, Wicken, Ely, Cambridgeshire CB7 5XR (01353) 721999
fax (01353) 724074 e-mail orders@privatecellar.co.uk website www.privatecellar.co.uk hours Mon–Fri 8–6
cards Delta, Maestro, MasterCard, Visa delivery £14.50, or free for orders of 24+ bottles or over £300 in mainland
England and Wales. Scotland, islands, Northern Ireland and worldwide, phone for quote en primeur Bordeaux, Burgundy,
Rhône, Germany, Port, California. C M T
✪ *Friendly, personal wine advice is part of the service; wines are predominantly French, with lots of 'everyday claret' at £10–15.*

Quaff Fine Wine Merchant

139–141 Portland Road, Hove BN3 5QJ (01273) 820320
fax (01273) 820326 e-mail sales@quaffit.com website www.quaffit.com
hours Mon–Thurs 10.30–7.30, Fri–Sat 10–8, Sun 12–7 cards Access, Maestro, MasterCard, Visa
discounts 10% mixed case delivery Next working day nationwide, charge depends on order value. C G M T
✪ *Extensive and keenly priced list organized by grape variety rather than country.*

Raeburn Fine Wines

21–23 Comely Bank Road, Edinburgh EH4 1DS (0131) 343 1159
fax (0131) 332 5166 e-mail sales@raeburnfinewines.com website www.raeburnfinewines.com
hours Mon–Sat 9.30–6 cards AmEx, Maestro, MasterCard, Visa discounts 5% unsplit case, 2.5% mixed
delivery Free local area 1 or more cases (usually); elsewhere at cost en primeur Australia, Bordeaux, Burgundy,
California, Germany, Italy, Languedoc-Roussillon, Loire, New Zealand, Rhône. G M T
✪ *Carefully chosen list, mainly from small growers. Italy and France – especially Burgundy – are specialities,
with Germany, Austria and northern Spain close behind, as well as selected Port and sought-after California wines.*

Real Wine Co.

mail order 1 Cannon Meadow, Bull Lane, Gerrards Cross, Buckinghamshire SL9 8RE (01753) 885619
e-mail mark@therealwineco.co.uk website www.therealwineco.co.uk cards Delta, Maestro, MasterCard, Visa
delivery £6.99 per order, orders over £250 free minimum order 1 mixed case.
✪ *Owner Mark Hughes has based his list entirely on his personal taste – check it out and see if you agree with
his lively tasting notes. There are plenty of good-value wines, including several rosés.*

Reid Wines

The Mill, Marsh Lane, Hallatrow, Nr Bristol BS39 6EB (01761) 452645
fax (01761) 453642 e-mail reidwines@aol.com hours Mon–Fri 9–5.30
cards Access, Maestro, MasterCard, Visa (3% charge) delivery Free within 25 miles of Hallatrow (Bristol),
and in central London for orders over 2 cases en primeur Claret. C G M T
✪ *A mix of great old wines, some old duds and splendid current stuff. Italy, USA, Australia, port and Madeira look tremendous.*

Howard Ripley

mail order 25 Dingwall Road, London SW18 3AZ (020) 8877 3065
fax (020) 8877 0029 e-mail info@howardripley.com website www.howardripley.com
hours Mon–Fri 9–6, Sat 9–1 cards Maestro, MasterCard, Visa delivery Minimum charge £10.50 + VAT, free UK
mainland on orders over £500 ex-VAT minimum order 1 case en primeur Burgundy, Germany. C M T
✪ *A must-have list for serious Burgundy lovers; expensive but not excessive. The German range is also excellent.*

The following services are available where indicated: **C** = cellarage **G** = glass hire/loan **M** = mail/online order **T** = tastings and talks

Roberson

348 Kensington High Street, London W14 8NS (020) 7371 2121

fax (020) 7371 4010   e-mail retail@roberson.co.uk   website www.robersonwinemerchant.co.uk; www.roberson.co.uk

hours Mon–Sat 10–8, Sun 12–6   cards Access, AmEx, Maestro, MasterCard, Visa   discounts (mail order) 5% on champagne and spirits, 10% or wine cases   delivery Free delivery within London, otherwise £15 per case

en primeur Bordeaux, Port.   C G M T

✪ *Fine and rare wines, sold by the bottle. All of France is excellent; so is Italy and port. With friendly, knowledgeable staff, the shop is well worth a visit.*

The RSJ Wine Company

33 Coin Street, London SE1 9NR (020) 7928 4554

fax (020) 7928 9768   e-mail tom.king@rsj.uk.com   website www.rsj.uk.com

hours Mon–Fri 9–6, answering machine at other times   cards AmEx, Maestro, MasterCard, Visa   delivery Free central London, minimum 1 case; England and Wales (per case), £14.10 1 case, £10.25 2 cases or more.   G M T

✪ *A roll-call of great Loire names, and some good Bordeaux.*

Sainsbury's

head office 33 Holborn, London EC1N 2HT (020) 7695 6000

customer service 0800 636262; 800 stores

website www.sainsburys.co.uk   online groceries helpline 0800 328 1700

hours Variable, some 24 hrs, locals generally Mon–Sat 7–11, Sun 10 or 11–4   cards AmEx, Maestro, MasterCard, Visa

discounts 5% for 6 bottles or more.   G M T

✪ *A collection to cater for bargain hunters as well as lovers of good-value wine higher up the scale. They've expanded their Taste the Difference range and got some top producers on board.*

Savage Selection

The Ox House, Market Place, Northleach, Cheltenham, Glos GL54 3EG (01451) 860896

fax (01451) 860996 • The Ox House Shop and Wine Bar at same address (01451) 860680

e-mail wine@savageselection.co.uk   website www.savageselection.co.uk

hours Office Mon–Fri 9–6; shop and wine bar Tue–Sat 10–10   cards Maestro, MasterCard, Visa

delivery Free locally for orders over £100; elsewhere on UK mainland free for orders over £250; smaller orders £10 + VAT for 1 case and £5 + VAT for each additional case en primeur Bordeaux. C G M T

✪ *Owner Mark Savage MW seeks out wines of genuine originality and personality from small family estates in 16 countries. France is the mainstay, alongside wines from Slovenia, Austria, Oregon and elsewhere.*

Seckford Wines

Dock Lane, Melton, Suffolk IP12 1PE (01394) 446622

fax (01394) 446633 e-mail sales@seckfordwines.co.uk website www.seckfordwines.co.uk

cards Maestro, MasterCard, Visa delivery £13.80 per consignment in UK mainland; elsewhere at cost

minimum order 1 mixed case en primeur Bordeaux, Burgundy. C M

✪ *Bordeaux, Burgundy, Champagne and the Rhône are the stars of this list, with some excellent older vintages. Serious stuff from Italy and Spain, too.*

Selfridges

400 Oxford Street, London W1A 1AB 0800 123 400 (for all stores)

• Upper Mall East, Bullring, Birmingham B5 4BP

• 1 Exchange Square, Manchester M3 1BD

• The Trafford Centre, Manchester M17 8DA

fax (01394) 446633 e-mail wineshop@selfridges.co.uk website www.selfridges.com

hours London Mon–Sat 9.30–9, Sun 12–6; Birmingham Mon–Fri 10–8 (Thurs 10–9), Sat 9–8, Sun 11–5; Manchester branches Mon–Fri 10–8 (Thurs 10–9), Sat 9–8, Sun 11–5

cards Maestro, MasterCard, Visa discounts 10% case discount delivery Next day £10 within UK mainland. T

✪ *Strong fine wine list. Great selection for gifts and regular tastings.*

Somerfield See Co-operative Group

Sommelier Wine Co

23 St George's Esplanade, St Peter Port, Guernsey, Channel Islands, GY1 2BG (01481) 721677

fax (01481) 716818 hours Mon–Sat 9.15–5.30, except Fri 9.15–6 cards Maestro, MasterCard, Visa

discounts 5% 1 case or more delivery Free locally (minimum 1 mixed case); being outside the European Community and with Customs restrictions means that the shipping of wine to the UK mainland is not possible. G T

✪ *An excellent list, with interesting, unusual wines. A big selection of top-notch Australia, Italy, Loire, Beaujolais, Burgundy, Bordeaux, the Rhône, Spain and South Africa.*

Stainton Wines

1 Station Yard, Station Road, Kendal, Cumbria LA9 6BT (01539) 731886   fax (01539) 730396
e-mail admin@stainton-wines.co.uk   website www.stainton-wines.co.uk   hours Mon–Fri 9–5.30, Sat 9–4.30
cards Maestro, MasterCard, Visa   discounts 5% mixed case   delivery Free Cumbria and North Lancashire;
elsewhere (per case) £13 1 case, more than 1 case variable.   G M T
✪ The list includes some great Bordeaux, interesting Burgundy, and leading names from Italy and Chile.

Stevens Garnier

47 West Way, Botley, Oxford OX2 0JF (01865) 263303
fax (01865) 791594   e-mail shop@stevensgarnier.co.uk   hours Mon–Thur 10–6, Fri 10–7, Sat 10–5
cards AmEx, Maestro, MasterCard, Visa, Solo   discounts 10% on 12 bottles   delivery Free locally.   G M T
✪ Regional France is a strength: this is one of the few places in the UK you can buy wine from Savoie. Likewise,
there are interesting choices from Portugal, Australia, Chile and Canada.

Stone, Vine & Sun

mail order No. 13 Humphrey Farms, Hazeley Road, Twyford, Winchester SO21 1QA (01962) 712351
fax (01962) 717545   e-mail sales@stonevine.co.uk   website www.stonevine.co.uk
hours Mon–Fri 9–6, Sat 9.30–4   cards Access, Maestro, MasterCard, Visa   discounts 5% on an unmixed case
delivery £5 for 1st case, £8.50 for 2 cases, free for orders over £250. Prices vary for Scottish Highlands, islands
and Northern Ireland.   G M T
✪ Lovely list marked by enthusiasm and passion for the subject. Lots of interesting stuff from France,
but also from Germany, South Africa, New Zealand, Chile, Argentina and elsewhere.

Sunday Times Wine Club

mail order New Aquitaine House, Exeter Way, Theale, Reading, Berks RG7 4PL
order line 0870 220 0020   fax 0870 220 0030   e-mail orders@sundaytimeswineclub.co.uk
website www.sundaytimeswineclub.co.uk   hours Mon–Fri 8–11, Sat–Sun 8–9   cards AmEx, Diners, Maestro,
MasterCard, Visa   delivery £5.99 per order   en primeur Australia, Bordeaux, Burgundy, Rhône.   C M T
✪ Essentially the same as Laithwaites (see page 173), though the special offers come round at different times.
The membership fee is £10 per annum. The club runs tours and tasting events for its members.

The following services are available where indicated: C = cellarage **G** = glass hire/loan **M** = mail/online order **T** = tastings and talks

Swig

mail order/online 188 Sutton Court Road, London W4 3HR (020) 8995 7060 or freephone 08000 272 272
fax (020) 8995 6195 e-mail wine@swig.co.uk website www.swig.co.uk
cards Amex, MasterCard, Switch, Visa
minimum order 12 bottles delivery £9.50 per address en primeur Bordeaux, Burgundy, South Africa. C G M T
✪ *Seriously good wines sold in an unserious way. For instant recommendations there's a list of 'current favourites'
listed in price bands; there's lots between £8 and £20 and the list covers pretty much everything you might want.*

T & W Wines

5 Station Way, Brandon, Suffolk IP27 0BH (01842) 814414
fax (01842) 819967 e-mail contact@tw-wines.com website www.tw-wines.com
hours Mon–Fri 9–5.30, occasional Sat 9.30–1 cards AmEx, MasterCard, Visa
delivery (Most areas) 7–23 bottles £18.95 + VAT, 2 or more cases free en primeur Burgundy. C G M T
✪ *A good list, particularly if you're looking for Burgundy, Rhône, Alsace or the Loire, but prices are not especially low.*

Tanners

26 Wyle Cop, Shrewsbury, Shropshire SY1 1XD (01743) 234500 fax (01743) 234501
• 36 High Street, Bridgnorth WV16 4DB (01746) 763148 fax (01746) 769798
• 4 St Peter's Square, Hereford HR1 2PG (01432) 272044 fax (01432) 263316
• Council Street West, Llandudno LL30 1ED (01492) 874099 fax (01492) 874788
• Severn Farm Enterprise Park, Welshpool SY21 7DF (01938) 552542 fax (01938) 556565
e-mail sales@tanners-wines.co.uk website www.tanners-wines.co.uk hours Shrewsbury Mon–Sat 9–6, branches
9–5.30 cards Maestro, MasterCard, Visa discounts 5% 1 mixed case, 7.5% 3 mixed cases (cash & collection);
5% for 3 mixed cases, 7.5% for 5 (mail order) delivery Free on orders over £90 to one address, otherwise £7.50
minimum order £25 en primeur Bordeaux, Burgundy, Rhône, Germany, Port, occasionally others. C G M T
✪ *Outstanding, award-winning merchant: Bordeaux, Burgundy and Germany are terrific.*

Tesco

head office Tesco House, PO Box 18, Delamare Road, Cheshunt EN8 9SL (01992) 632222
fax (01992) 630794 customer service 0800 505555; 1830 licensed branches e-mail customer.services@tesco.co.uk
website www.tesco.com hours Variable cards Maestro, MasterCard, Visa
discount 5% on 6 bottles or more. G M T

• Calais store Tesco Vin Plus, Cité Europe, 122 Boulevard du Kent, 62231 Coquelles, France (00 33) 3 21 46 02 70 website www.tesco.com/vinplus; www.tesco-france.com hours Mon–Sat 8.30am–10pm

✪ Premium wines at around £20 down to bargain basement bottles. Tesco.com has an even greater selection by the case.

Threshers See Wine Rack.

Turville Valley Wines

The Firs, Potter Row, Great Missenden, Bucks HP16 9LT (01494) 868818
fax (01494) 868832 e-mail chris@turville-valley-wines.com website www.turville-valley-wines.com
hours Mon–Fri 9–5.30 cards None delivery By arrangement minimum order £300 excluding VAT/12 bottles. C M

✪ Top-quality fine and rare wines at trade prices.

Valvona & Crolla

19 Elm Row, Edinburgh EH7 4AA (0131) 556 6066 fax (0131) 556 1668
e-mail wine@valvonacrolla.co.uk website www.valvonacrolla.co.uk
hours Shop: Mon–Sat 8.30–6, Sun 10.30–4.30, Caffe bar: Mon–Sat 8.30–5.30, Sun 10.30–4 cards AmEx, Maestro,
MasterCard, Visa discounts 7% 1–3 cases, 10% 4 or more delivery Free on orders over £150, otherwise £9; Saturday
mornings free on orders over £200, otherwise £25. M T

✪ Exciting selection of wines from all over the world, but specializing in Italy, including Puglia, Sicily and Sardinia.

Villeneuve Wines

1 Venlaw Court, Peebles, Scotland EH45 8AE (01721) 722500 fax (01721) 729922
• 82 High Street, Haddington EH41 3ET (01620) 822224 • 49A Broughton Street, Edinburgh EH1 3RJ (0131) 558 8441
e-mail wines@villeneuvewines.com website www.villeneuvewines.com
hours (Peebles) Mon–Sat 9–8, Sun 12.30–5.30; (Haddington) Mon–Sat 9–7; (Edinburgh) Mon–Wed 12.30–10,
Thurs 10–10, Fri–Sat 9–10, Sun 12.30–10 cards AmEx, Maestro, MasterCard, Visa
delivery Free locally, £8.50 per case elsewhere. G M T

✪ Italy, Australia and New Zealand are all marvellous here. France is good and Spain is clearly an enthusiasm, too.

Vin du Van

mail order Colthups, The Street, Appledore, Kent TN26 2BX (01233) 758727 fax (01233) 758389
hours Mon–Fri 9–5 cards Delta, Maestro, MasterCard, Visa delivery Free locally; elsewhere £5.95 for first case,

further cases free. Highlands and islands, ask for quote minimum order 1 mixed case. M

○ *Extensive, wonderfully quirky, star-studded Australian list; the kind of inspired lunacy I'd take to read on a desert island.*

Vinceremos

mail order Munro House, Duke Street, Leeds LS9 8AG 0800 107 3086 fax (0113) 288 4566
e-mail info@vinceremos.co.uk website www.vinceremos.co.uk hours Mon–Fri 8.30–5.30
cards AmEx, Delta, Maestro, MasterCard, Visa discounts 5% on 5 cases or more, 10% on 10 cases or more
delivery Free 5 cases or more. M

○ *Organic specialist, with a wide-ranging list of wines, including biodynamic and Fairtrade.*

Vintage Roots

mail order Holdshott Farm, Reading Road, Heckfield, Hook, Hampshire, RG27 0JZ (0118) 932 6566 fax (0118) 922 5115
hours Mon–Fri 8.30–5.30, Saturdays in December e-mail info@vintageroots.co.uk website www.vintageroots.co.uk
cards Delta, Maestro, MasterCard, Visa discounts 5% on 5 cases or over delivery £6.95 for any delivery under 5 cases;
more than 6 cases is free. Some local deliveries free. Cases can be mixed. G M T

○ *Everything on this list is certified organic and/or biodynamic, from Champagne and other fizz to beer and cider.*

Virgin Wines

mail order The Loft, St James' Mill, Whitefriars, Norwich NR3 1TN 0870 164 9593
fax (01603) 619277 e-mail help@virginwines.com website www.virginwines.com
hours (Office) Mon–Fri 8.30–6, Sat 9–1 cards AmEx, Maestro, MasterCard, Visa
delivery £6.99 per order for all UK deliveries minimum order 1 case. M T

○ *Online retailer with reasonably priced wines from all over the world. Well-balanced pre-mixed cases,
or you can mix your own.*

Waitrose

head office Doncastle Road, Southern Industrial Area, Bracknell, Berkshire RG12 8YA
customer service 0800 188884, 212 licensed stores e-mail customer_service@waitrose.co.uk
website www.waitrosewine.com hours Mon–Sat 8.30–7, 8 or 9, Sun 10–4 or 11–5
cards AmEx, Delta, Maestro, MasterCard, Partnership Card, Visa
discounts Regular monthly promotions, 5% off for 6 bottles or more
home delivery Available through www.waitrosedeliver.com and www.ocado.com and Waitrose Wine Direct (*overleaf*)

en primeur Bordeaux and Burgundy available through Waitrose Wine Direct. G T

• waitrose wine direct order online at www.waitrosewine.com or 0800 188881

e-mail wineadvisor@johnlewis.com discounts Vary monthly on featured cases; branch promotions are matched. All cases include a 5% discount to match branch offer.

delivery Free standard delivery throughout UK mainland, Northern Ireland and Isle of Wight. Named day delivery, £6.95 per addressee (order by 6pm for next day – not Sun); next-day delivery before 10.30am, £9.95 per addressee (order by 6pm for next working day).

✪ *Ahead of the other supermarkets in quality, value and imagination. Still lots of tasty stuff under £5.*

Waterloo Wine Co

office and warehouse 6 Vine Yard, London SE1 1QL shop 59–61 Lant Street, London SE1 1QN (020) 7403 7967

fax (020) 7357 6976 e-mail sales@waterloowine.co.uk website www.waterloowine.co.uk

hours Mon–Fri 11–7.30, Sat 10–5 cards AmEx, Maestro, MasterCard, Visa

delivery Free 5 cases in central London (otherwise £5); elsewhere, 1 case £12, 2 cases £7.50 each. G T

✪ *Quirky, personal list, strong in the Loire and New Zealand.*

Wimbledon Wine Cellar

1 Gladstone Road, Wimbledon, London SW19 1QU (020) 8540 9979 fax (020) 8540 9399

• 84 Chiswick High Road, London W4 1SY (020) 8994 7989 fax (020) 8994 3683

• 4 The Boulevard, Imperial Wharf, Chelsea, London SW6 2UB (020) 7736 2191

e-mail enquiries@wimbledonwinecellar.com, chiswick@wimbledonwinecellar.com or chelsea@wimbledonwinecellar.com website www.wimbledonwinecellar.com

hours Mon–Sat 10–9; Sun 11–7 (Chelsea only) cards AmEx, Maestro, MasterCard, Visa

discounts 10% off 1 case (with a few exceptions), 20% off case of 6 Champagne

delivery Free local delivery. Courier charges elsewhere en primeur Burgundy, Bordeaux, Tuscany, Rhône. C G M T

✪ *Top names from Italy, Burgundy, Bordeaux, Rhône, Loire – and some of the best of the New World.*

Wine & Beer World (Majestic)

head office Majestic House, Otterspool Way, Watford, Herts WD25 8WW (01923) 298200

e-mail info@wineandbeer.co.uk website www.majestic.co.uk

• Rue du Judée, Zone Marcel Doret, Calais 62100, France (0033) 3 21 97 63 00 email calais@majestic.co.uk

• Centre Commercial Carrefour, Quai L'Entrepôt, Cherbourg 50100, France (0033) 2 33 22 23 22 email cherbourg@majestic.co.uk
• Unit 3A, Zone La Française, Coquelles 62331, France (0033) 3 21 82 93 64 email coquelles@majestic.co.uk
pre-order (01923) 298297. Free ferry crossing from Dover to Calais when your pre-order is over £400
hours (Calais) 7 days 8–8; (Cherbourg) Mon–Sat 9–7; (Coquelles) 7 days 8.30–7; Calais and Coquelles open Bank
Holidays cards Maestro, MasterCard, Visa. T
✪ *The French arm of Majestic, with savings of up to 50% on UK prices. Calais is the largest branch and Coquelles the nearest to the Channel Tunnel terminal. English-speaking staff.*

The Wine Company
mail order Town Barton, Doddiscombsleigh, Nr Exeter, Devon EX6 7PT (01647) 252005
e-mail nick@thewinecompany.biz website www.thewinecompany.biz hours Mon–Sun 9–6
cards AmEx, Maestro, MasterCard, Visa delivery £7.99 per case, free for orders over £150, UK mainland only. M
✪ *The list of around 250 wines specializes in Australia and South Africa, with some top names you won't find anywhere else.*

Wine Rack (First Quench Retailing, Haddows, The Local, Thresher Wine Shops)
head office FQR House, Bessemer Road, Welwyn Garden City, Herts AL7 1BL (01707) 387200
fax (01707) 387350 website www.winerack.co.uk; 370 Wine Rack stores, 382 Thresher Wine Shops,
491 The Local, 100 Haddows stores hours Mon–Sat 10–10 (some 10.30), Sun 11–10, Scotland 12.30–10.30
cards Maestro, MasterCard, Visa delivery Free locally, some branches. G T
✪ *New Zealand and France take the leading roles, with strong support from Australia, Spain and Italy. The popular 3 for 2 deal means you'll get some real bargains if you buy any 3 bottles – but some single bottle prices are on the high side.*

The Wine Society
mail order Gunnels Wood Road, Stevenage, Herts SG1 2BG (01438) 741177
fax (01438) 761167 order line (01438) 740222 e-mail memberservices@thewinesociety.com
website www.thewinesociety.com
hours Mon–Fri 8.30–9, Sat 9–5; showroom: Mon–Fri 10–6, Thurs 10–7, Sat 9.30–5.30
cards Delta, Maestro, MasterCard, Visa discounts (per case) £3 for pre-ordered collection delivery Free 1 case or more
anywhere in UK; also collection facility at Templepatrick, County Antrim, and showroom and collection facility at Montreuil,
France, at French rates of duty and VAT en primeur Bordeaux, Burgundy, Germany, Port, Rhône.
✪ *An outstanding list from an inspired wine-buying team. Masses of well-chosen affordable wines as well as big names.*

The Wine Treasury

mail order 69–71 Bondway, London SW8 1SQ (020) 7793 9999

fax (020) 7793 8080 e-mail bottled@winetreasury.com website www.winetreasury.com hours Mon–Fri 9.30–6

cards Maestro, MasterCard, Visa discounts 10% for unmixed dozens delivery Free for orders over £200, England and Wales; Scotland phone for more details minimum order 1 mixed case. M

✪ *Excellent choices and top names from California and Italy – but they don't come cheap.*

Winemark the Wine Merchants

3 Duncrue Place, Belfast BT3 9BU (028) 9074 6274 fax (028) 9074 8022; 77 branches e-mail info@winemark.com

website www.winemark.com hours Branches vary, but in general Mon–Sat 10–10, Sun 12–8

cards Switch, MasterCard, Visa discounts 5% on 6–11 bottles, 10% on 12 bottles or more. G M T

✪ *Over 500 wines, with some interesting wines from Australia, New Zealand, Chile and California.*

The Winery

4 Clifton Road, London W9 1SS (020) 7286 6475 fax (020) 7286 2733 e-mail info@thewineryuk.com

website www.thewineryuk.com hours Mon–Sat 11–9.30, Sun and public holidays 12–8 cards Maestro, MasterCard, Visa discounts 5% on a mixed case delivery Free locally or for 3 cases or more, otherwise £10 per case. G M T

✪ *Largest selection of dry German wines in the UK. Burgundy, Rhône, Champagne, Italy and California are other specialities.*

Wines of Westhorpe

mail order 136a Doncaster Road, Mexborough, South Yorkshire S64 0JW (01709) 584863 fax (01709) 584863

e-mail wines@westhorpe.co.uk website www.westhorpe.co.uk hours Mon–Thu 9–8, Fri–Sat 9–6

cards Maestro, MasterCard, Visa discounts Variable on 2 dozen or more delivery Free UK mainland (except northern Scotland) minimum order 1 mixed case. M

✪ *An excellent list for devotees of Eastern European wines – especially Hungarian and Romanian – all at reasonable prices.*

WoodWinters

16 Henderson Street, Bridge of Allan, Scotland, FK9 4HP (01786) 834894

e-mail shop@woodwinters.com website www.woodwinters.com hours Mon–Sat 10am–7pm; Sun 1–5pm

cards MasterCard, Switch, Visa discounts Vintners Dozen: buy 12 items or more and get a 13th free – we are happy to choose something appropriate for you delivery £8.95 per address; free for orders over £150 UK mainland. Islands and Northern Ireland, phone for quote en primeur Bordeaux, Burgundy, Italy, Rhone. C G M T

✪ *A young, ambitious operation, very strong on California and Australia, but also good stuff from Austria, Portugal, Italy, Spain and Burgundy. They do like flavour, so expect most of their wines to be mouth-filling. Wine tasting club and courses.*

Wright Wine Co
The Old Smithy, Raikes Road, Skipton, North Yorkshire BD23 1NP (01756) 700886 (01756) 794175 fax (01756) 798580 e-mail sales@wineandwhisky.co.uk website www.wineandwhisky.co.uk hours Mon–Fri 9–6; Sat 10–5:30; open Sundays in December 10.30–4 cards Maestro, MasterCard, Visa discounts 10% unsplit case, 5% mixed case delivery Free within 30 miles, elsewhere at cost. G
✪ *Equally good in both Old World and New World, with plenty of good stuff at keen prices. Wide choice of half bottles.*

Peter Wylie Fine Wines
Plymtree Manor, Plymtree, Cullompton, Devon EX15 2LE (01884) 277555 fax (01884) 277557 e-mail peter@wyliefinewines.co.uk website www.wyliefinewines.co.uk hours Mon–Fri 9–6 discounts Only on unsplit cases delivery Up to 3 cases in London £26, otherwise by arrangement. C M
✪ *Fascinating list of mature wines: Bordeaux from throughout the 20th century, vintage ports going back to 1908.*

Yapp Brothers
shop The Old Brewery, Water Street, Mere, Wilts BA12 6DY (01747) 860423 fax (01747) 860929 e-mail sales@yapp.co.uk website www.yapp.co.uk hours Mon–Sat 9–6 cards Maestro, MasterCard, Visa discounts £6 per case on collection delivery £8 one case, 2 or more cases free. C G M T
✪ *Rhône and Loire specialists. Also some of the hard-to-find wines of Provence, Savoie, South-West France and Corsica.*

Noel Young Wines
56 High Street, Trumpington, Cambridge CB2 9LS (01223) 566744 fax (01223) 844736 e-mail admin@nywines.co.uk website www.nywines.co.uk hours Mon–Fri 10–8, Sat 10–7, Sun 12–2 cards AmEx, Maestro, MasterCard, Visa discounts 5% for orders over £500 delivery Free over 12 bottles unless discounted en primeur Australia, Burgundy, Italy, Rhône. G M T
✪ *Fantastic wines from just about everywhere. Australia is a particular passion and there is a great Austrian list, some terrific Germans, plus beautiful Burgundies, Italians and dessert wines.*

The following services are available where indicated: **C** = cellarage **G** = glass hire/loan **M** = mail/online order **T** = tastings and talks

Who's where

COUNTRYWIDE/MAIL
ORDER/ONLINE
Adnams
Aldi
ASDA
AustralianWineCentre.co
.uk
H & H Bancroft Wines
Bibendum Wine
Big Red Wine Co
Bordeaux Index
Anthony Byrne
ChateauOnline
Chilean Wine Club
Co-op
Croque-en-Bouche
Devigne Wines
Nick Dobson Wines
Domaine Direct
FromVineyardsDirect.com
Roger Harris Wines
Jeroboams
Justerini & Brooks
Laithwaites
Lay & Wheeler
Laytons
Liberty Wines
O W Loeb
Majestic
Marks & Spencer
Millésima
Montrachet
Morrisons
New Zealand House of
Wine
Oddbins
OZ WINES
Private Cellar
Real Wine Co

Howard Ripley
Sainsbury's
Stone, Vine & Sun
Sunday Times Wine Club
Swig
Tesco
Thresher
Vin du Van
Vinceremos
Vintage Roots
Virgin Wines
Waitrose
The Wine Company
Wine Rack
The Wine Society
The Wine Treasury
Wines of Westhorpe
Peter Wylie Fine Wines
Yapp Brothers
Noel Young Wines

LONDON
Armit
Balls Brothers
Berkmann Wine Cellars
Berry Bros. & Rudd
Budgens
Corney & Barrow
Farr Vintners
Fortnum & Mason
Friarwood
Goedhuis & Co
Green & Blue
Handford Wines
Harvey Nichols
Haynes Hanson & Clark
Jeroboams
Lea & Sandeman
Moreno Wines

Philglas & Swiggot
Roberson
RSJ Wine Company
Selfridges
Waterloo Wine Co
Wimbledon Wine Cellar
The Winery

SOUTH-EAST AND
HOME COUNTIES
A&B Vintners
Berry Bros. & Rudd
Budgens
Butlers Wine Cellar
Les Caves de Pyrene
Flagship Wines
The Flying Corkscrew
Hedley Wright
Maison du Vin
Quaff
Turville Valley Wines

WEST AND
SOUTH-WEST
Averys Wine Merchants
Bennetts Fine Wines
Berkmann Wine Cellars
Great Western Wine
Haynes Hanson & Clark
Hicks & Don
Laymont & Shaw
Christopher Piper Wines
Reid Wines
Savage Selection
Peter Wylie Fine Wines
Yapp Brothers

EAST ANGLIA
Adnams

Budgens
Anthony Byrne
Cambridge Wine
Merchants
Colchester Wine Co
Corney & Barrow
Seckford Wines
T & W Wines
Noel Young Wines

MIDLANDS
Bat & Bottle
Connolly's
deFINE Food and Wine
Gauntleys
Harvey Nichols
S H Jones
Nickolls & Perks
Noble Rot Wine
Warehouses
Oxford Wine Co
Portland Wine Co
Selfridges
Stevens Garnier
Tanners

NORTH
Berkmann Wine Cellars
Booths
D Byrne
Great Northern Wine
Halifax Wine Co
Harvey Nichols
Martinez Wines
Nidderdale Fine Wines
Penistone Court Wine
Cellars
Playford Ros
Selfridges

Stainton Wines
Wright Wine Co

WALES
Ballantynes
Fingal-Rock
Terry Platt Wine
Merchants
Tanners

SCOTLAND
Cockburns of Leith
Corney & Barrow
Friarwood
Peter Green & Co
Harvey Nichols
Linlithgow Wines
Raeburn Fine Wines
Valvona & Crolla
Villeneuve Wines
WoodWinters

IRELAND
Direct Wine Shipments
James Nicholson
O'Briens
Winemark

CHANNEL ISLANDS
Sommelier Wine Co

FRANCE
ChateauOnline
Millésima
Oddbins
Tesco Vin Plus
Wine & Beer World